# RAISING
# Happy
# CHILDREN

**The key to a calm, connected child**

**LIZANNE DU PLESSIS**

Liewe Karin,

Vir die werk wat jy doen —
jy is 'n inspirasie!

Baie dankie,

Lizanne x

 METZ PRESS
www.metzpress.co.za

**THIS BOOK IS DEDICATED TO:**
*Lize and Cara*
I love you to the moon and back … trillion times

*Marius*
I admire you … always

*My Heavenly Father*
I worship you … forever

Published by Metz Press
1 Cameronians Avenue, Welgemoed 7530
South Africa

First published in 2014

Copyright © Metz Press 2014
Copyright text © Lizanne du Plessis
Illustrations copyright © Metz Press

Publisher: Wilsia Metz
Illustrations: Nikki Miles
Design: Liezl Maree
Proofreader: Carla Masson
Print production: Andrew de Kock
Printed and bound by Paarl Media, 15 Van Riebeeck Road, Paarl

ISBN 978-1-928201-16-8

# CONTENTS

# PREFACE

*"How do you spell 'love'?"* – Piglet
*"You don't spell it … you feel it."* – Pooh

– A.A. Milne, *Winnie-the-Pooh*

## I believe that parenting is all about the relationship

Parenting is great – it is definitely the most significant journey I've ever been on. But, oh boy, it has also been the most challenging and demanding experience ever! Becoming a mum rocked my world. It turned everything I knew, or at least everything I thought I knew, upside down. Have *you* ever felt overwhelmed, exhausted and disillusioned as a parent? I have. Not once, not ten times, probably at least once a week – overcome with uncertainty, self-doubt, shame, blame and guilt. At times I felt vulnerable to the bone. I would ask myself *why nobody told me that being a parent was going to be this hard?* Of course, the truth is that it wouldn't have made any difference. It is only when you *become* a parent that you truly feel and really understand what it means. I never expected it to be so easy and so hard – all at the same time. Sometimes I feel I might pop with excitement and love and compassion, but then there are the times when things get messy … and I have to work very hard at keeping it all together. It took years before I realised that it is not possible for parents to keep it all together all the time. It is only by embracing the imperfection that comes with parenthood that we are able to move forward. I had to accept that it is okay if things get messy; that perfect parenthood is a dangerous myth. When striving for perfection we sacrifice joy, compassion and connection in our lives.

I always wanted to get married (to a prince on a white horse, of course), have children and be the best mum I could possibly be. My dreams became reality when God blessed me with falling pregnant against all odds and a 1.8-kilogram baby girl was born at 34 weeks. With the help of my loving husband and supportive mother and sister, we did skin-to-skin (kangaroo care) with her for almost four weeks. Nearly four years later, after yet another miracle, I was pregnant with my second child. With her birth we were expats in the Netherlands and shortly thereafter moved to London.

Our parenting journey has been a rollercoaster ride with lots of ups and downs and many opportunities for personal growth and learning. Then came the day when time stood still for a few minutes – when the business of trying to do it all became unbearable. My youngest daughter, Cara, was 18 months old and running a temperature throughout the day. About 45 minutes after putting her down for the night, my husband heard an unfamiliar sound on the baby monitor and went to check on her. Within a few seconds, he shouted for help. Cara was fitting and not breathing. I literally felt my world spinning and remember little of what followed. Cara suffered a febrile convulsion resulting from an underlying ear infection that caused her temperature to spike. I later learnt that it is relatively common in childhood and not serious. Cara was back to her old self within a few hours, but that experience changed me forever. I got my wake-up call in the ambulance, looking at her lifeless body, wondering if she'll ever open her eyes again, if she'll ever be able to talk, walk and think again. It was in that moment of complete and utter vulnerability that I realised that what matters most is the bond of love and connection we have with our children. Being an imperfect mum in this broken world is as whole as it will ever get.

In the weeks thereafter, while processing this traumatic event, I made a conscious decision to stop trying to be a supermum, and rather to be *an intentional mum*. For me that has been one of the most empowering experiences ever. I felt overcome with relief. I was set free. I could allow myself to be vulnerable and simply place love, compassion and my relationship with my children above all else. I decided to be a conscious, aware and deliberate parent – not perfect. I gave myself permission to make mistakes, to get it wrong and then to get up, be brave and move on. One step at a time.

Often this is much easier said than done, though. The demands of the 21ˢᵗ century are huge. Never before have we had so much competing for our attention and getting in the way of our relationships with our children. We are under constant pressure to achieve results, over-scheduling our lives, packing more into a day than is humanly possible and expecting our children to perform at levels which are detrimental to their physical and emotional wellbeing. It's hard. But that doesn't mean that it's impossible. Now is the time to focus on building and strengthening deep, meaningful, heartfelt connections with our children.

> *"It is okay if things get messy.*
> *Perfect parenthood is a dangerous myth."*

Parenting is often presented as a skill that is supposed to come naturally, instinctively. We are made to believe that, as soon as we become a mother, our maternal instinct will kick in and, as if by magic, we will know how to parent. We hear about those wonderful feel-good hormones (oxytocin and opioids) that are released after birth and are responsible for activating the areas in the brain needed for attachment, love and responsiveness. But for some these feel-good hormones aren't enough to fall in love with their babies. And even if we love our children, truly love them like only parents can love their children, there are times when knowing what to do and how to do it will just not come naturally. Then the connection and relationships suffer. We become disengaged. We fall into the trap of self-doubt. *Nurture shock* is the term used to describe the panic that is common among new parents when they realise that the mythical fountain of parenting know-how does not start to flow as if by magic.

That is why I wrote this book. Like all relationships, your relationship with your child requires basic ingredients such as compassion, kindness, humility, gentleness and patience (see Colossians 3:12). I don't know about you, but having compassion and patience with my kids come much easier when I understand *how* their brains are wired. When I remind myself that they are developing kids, each with a unique temperament. It's more forgiving. I'm more forgiving.

So understanding comes first. Add to that the good old stuff that we know children need; nurturing rituals and flexible routines, intentional discipline and fun and laughter. The result is a strong, deep connection.

I have dragged my husband along on this intentional parenting ride (to be honest, he didn't have much choice in the matter). Now, after nearly 11 years of being parents, I can honestly say that he is as intentional about being a dad as he is about his job, his relationship with God and our marriage – if not more so. When he turns off the cricket and tells our girls that it's time to swing, mumbling something along the lines of, "You need some movement to regulate you," I get that warm, fuzzy feeling inside. We certainly don't feel that we have all the answers or know how to best handle our girls every single moment. They seem to develop, surprise and challenge us every day. There are days and times when we look at each other and ask, "What now?" We stumble, we fall and we constantly have to change direction. But one thing is certain – we both have the desire to be as conscious, aware and deliberate about our parenting as we possibly can.

I encourage you to drop your supermum cape and embrace humility and vulnerability. Let's walk this journey together. My wish is that the information in this book will give you the tools to build a strong and meaningful connection with your child.

# INTRODUCTION

*"Promise me you'll always remember: You're braver than you believe, and stronger than you seem, and smarter than you think."*

— A.A. Milne, *Winnie-the-Pooh*

## Why you need to read this book

From the moment that you hear you are pregnant, we as mums start dreaming about that little baby. Right? Even if you feel too vulnerable to share all your intimate thoughts, that's what we do. Most of us will agree that next to being healthy, our biggest dream and wish for our children, is for them to be happy. Happiness is something we might struggle to put our finger on. Is it a feeling, a thought or a place? We might describe it as being content, feeling joyful, flourishing and a general sense of wellbeing. Great news is that science is telling us that happiness is not something that you are born with (or without, for that matter). A part of it is genetically determined, but perhaps the biggest part of being happy is a combination of our environment and our ability to manage our own thoughts and feelings. That is where parenting comes into the mix. Raising happy children means raising children who are able to:
• regulate their bodies;
• manage big, overwhelming feelings; and
• develop their thinking.

Children are born with the *capacity* to do all this, but it takes time. Dr Christopher Green describes it brilliantly when he says: *"Toddlers are built to a design that is perfect in every detail, but for one small defect – they have all the activity of an international airport, but the control tower doesn't work."* But don't despair; your toddler is working very hard on getting that control tower to work. At first he will need you to help him, but with continued coaching, by the time he goes to school, he'll be able to operate that control tower much more independently. And all through a process – a highly complex and sophisticated one – called self-regulation.

**My mission is to empower you** – to give you the tools you need to play an active part in this process of your child's development. Part of this process is making sense of how your child is wired, because it is within his unique temperament that he will develop and within this understanding that you will be able to build a strong connection.

*"Being understood by a person we love is one of the most powerful yearnings, for adults and children alike. The need for understanding is part of what makes us human."* (Claudia Gold)

In this book I have used my experience as a mother and occupational therapist, combine it with the theory of neuroscience, developmental psychology and sensory processing. You do not need any fancy equipment for any of the suggested activities. I suggest ways for you to connect with, accept, support and love your child during your normal moment-to-moment interactions. My wish is that this will encourage you to:

- Change some of your ideas about why your child behaves in certain ways.
- Make adjustments in your home environment, routines and ways of interacting with your child.
- Forge a deep connection with your child that serves as the foundation for healthy development and a happy child.

But bear in mind that sustainable change doesn't happen overnight – the name of the game is baby steps.

Every sentence was written to achieve the following goals:

- Help you to **understand** your child.
- Give clear, concise and **practical suggestions** for day-to-day interactions.
- Give advice on how to **manage challenges** that cross your parenting path.

*Understanding why our kids do things the way they do, what makes them excited and what calms them down builds relationships, ensures healthy development and results in happy children.*

After reading this book you may see behaviour in a different light. You might think twice before you label your child as being naughty, defiant, hyper or fussy. Perhaps he is moaning because he has not had enough movement today? Perhaps he needs a nap or a snack or just some down time? Understanding your child's unique temperament will help you find ways to deal with his behaviour. Not only that – when you help your child to correctly interpret why he feels and behaves the way he does, you are increasing his self-awareness, his self-esteem and his self-love.

Three key concepts are deeply woven into the book and you will encounter them repeatedly. So let me briefly explain them:

## Unique sensory temperament

Everybody has a distinctive way of responding to sensory information and therefore a unique sensory temperament. Every child's personality, intellect and temperament are unique to him. **And that is why there is no one-size-fits-all recipe in raising happy children.** Even children from the same family growing up in the same environment vary in temperament and their ability to learn how to self-regulate (see below). Developing an understanding of your child's unique sensory temperament and how it affects his behaviour is critical.

    **The way that your child is wired to process sensory input accounts for her sensory temperament and is central to her behaviour.** Some children are social, alert and on the move, others are laid-back, easy-going and very adjustable, while others are sensitive, attentive and thoughtful. I like to think of the three unique sensory temperaments as personified by monkeys, giraffes and hedgehogs (more about that later).

## Self-regulation

Some call it self-control. Others say it is the way we react. No matter what you call it, self-regulation is something we do all the time (whether we are aware of it or not). With time your child's brain will mature. Through this and a loving parent-child relationship, your child will develop the ability to self-regulate. She will learn how to:

- regulate her body (so that she doesn't feel too sluggish or too revved up);
- manage overwhelming feelings (such as excitement, frustration, anger and fear); and
- mature her thinking (so that she is not ruled by her feelings alone).

Developing self-regulation, however, doesn't come as naturally to some children as to others. Some children need more help (coaching and practising) when it comes to learning and developing effective self-regulation skills. A great deal depends on the child's unique temperament. And let's not forget the environment in which the child grows up and the activities to which he is exposed. Understanding how your child's body and brain are uniquely wired, and how they develop as he grows, is the key.

> The ability to self-regulate is considered an essential part of children's healthy emotional development and is increasingly regarded as a good predictor of a child's academic success.

## Dysregulation

Dysregulation is the opposite of regulation. It happens when the body and brain are out of sync. "Losing it", "out of control", "hyper", "shutting down", "messy", "becoming unglued" are all terms that imply dysregulation.

🔑 *The goal is not to get rid of dysregulation. It is to understand where it is coming from, what it looks like and how to move through it.*

# How to read this book

Busy parents, busy toddlers and busy schedules … I know all about it. It is highly unlikely that you will read this book from start to finish, page by page. There are at least five parenting and personal development books on my night stand and I dip in and out of them as time allows. In all likelihood, this is what you do too. Therefore I will give you an overview of what you can expect in each section of the book, so that you can choose how to use it:

• **The preface and the introduction** told you about the person behind the words. I share my story, my values and my mission when writing the book. I explain key terminology and concepts that form the backbone of the book. So do start with this section.

• **Part I** provides information about your child's sensory body, and includes some fun games for you to do at home. When you read the section on your child's developing brain, you will discover things that you never knew before – I guarantee that it will be an enlightening read. Moving on you will learn about your child's unique sensory temperament – this will change the way you look at her forever. Sensory temperament applies to adults as well – you and your spouse or partner also have unique sensory temperaments and this may differ from each other's and from your children's (thank goodness, otherwise life and relationships would be very boring). So read through the entire chapter to get a good grasp of what types of behaviour describe the different temperaments. It might just come in handy in the future.

• **Part II** is about the nuts and bolts of self-regulation. You will discover the tools for raising calm, connected and joyful children. Knowing how to calm your child and having lots of activities to do at home, in the car, in the garden and in the queue at the shop will empower you to support your child in the development of this vital skill.

• **Part III** deals with the tough and challenging times. I discuss the whats, hows and whys of fear, anxiety and stress, the meltdowns and the dreaded tantrums. There are loads of practical advice to help you find ways to deal with the inevitable.

• **Part IV** will give you tools for intentional parenting on a daily basis. I talk about creating nurturing rituals and predictable routines from which toddlers benefit enormously. I also discuss the sticky subject of discipline and boundaries. And finally I get on my soapbox and share my thoughts on the importance of looking after yourself. Read this section for practical advice, because loving yourself is a prerequisite for loving your child.

Finally, since we are all in this together, I'd also like to get to know *you*, hear about your triumphs and challenges on the road to becoming an intentional parent and raising a happy child. Connect with me via www.lizanneduplessis.com.

# PART I

...........................................

# Getting to know your child

# Your child's sensory body

· · · · · · · · · · · · · · · · · · · · · · · · · · · · · · · · · · · · · · · · · · · · · · · ·

*"And I'd say to myself as I looked so lazily*
*down at the sea:*
*"There's nobody else in the world, and the*
*world was made for me."*
— A.A. Milne, *Winnie-the-Pooh*

We live in an amazing world filled with sensations. We are bombarded with sights, sounds, smells and movements from the moment we open our eyes until we go to bed at night (and it doesn't stop there, we are just not aware of it). What we *feel* through our senses, whether physically or emotionally, guides our *behaviour*. **Your child is showing you every day how his senses are doing – through the way he moves, plays and interacts.** His behaviour provides important clues to what is going on in his body and brain. Just as your child's fingerprints are unique to him, his brain is uniquely wired to make sense of all the incoming information. Because his body and brain develop over time, what bothers him today might not bother him tomorrow and his intense need for movement might lessen over time. How he responds to sensations and the world around him also depends on his age, the environment and the time of day.

In this chapter we'll explore:
- The eight senses (yes there are eight, not only five!)
- Why the senses matter
- Everyday activities for every sense
- How it all comes together (with a process called sensory processing).

# Our senses keep us alive, safe and active

Children learn, develop and interact with their world through seeing, hearing, smelling, feeling and moving. Apart from building critical pathways in the brain necessary for learning, their senses also *keep them safe and help them enjoy life to its fullest.*

Our senses help us to *engage and to be active and social.* If we like the feel or look of something, we want more of it. If you enjoy the experience of sinking into a hot bath, you'll look forward to it after a hard day. When a sensation makes us feel uncomfortable, we might ignore or avoid it. I refuse to go on any fast adventure ride with my children – to me that is just torture and I will avoid it at any cost.

Our senses also *keep us safe.* When our brains detect a threat, we literally "sense" danger and respond instinctively to protect ourselves, without having to think about it. We smell burning, realise it's the toast and respond by pressing the stop button on the toaster. We hear a car approaching and quickly step out of the road and onto the sidewalk. Our senses help us to survive.

> Abi has just mastered the art of propelling and steering her brand-new scooter. She smiles, gets on her scooter and whizzes off. What we don't see is how hard her body and brain are working. Her **senses of touch**, **movement** and **body position** enable her to hold onto the handlebars – not too tightly and not too loosely. Her **visual sense** guides her as she manoeuvres her scooter over and around obstacles. Her **movement sense** allows her to balance on one leg and her sense of **body position** enables her to judge the force with which she is propelling the scooter. Abi stops when she **hears** her mum calling. With practice she gets better and better until she doesn't have to think consciously about propelling and steering the scooter at all. Her brain forms important pathways enabling her to get on and go.

We seldom use just one sense at a time – little Abi uses many of her senses when riding her scooter. Complex tasks require involvement of all the senses through an intricate filtering and organising process. Each sense has a special job. It is important to understand these and also how they all work together, as it is the foundation for healthy development.

# Not five senses but eight!

Humans have eight senses – five are commonly known, but there are another three which you may not have heard of. All the senses work together and enable us to "take in" information from our body and the world around us.

The **five commonly known senses** are:
· **Touch**
· **Hearing**
· **Smell**
· **Taste**
· **Sight**

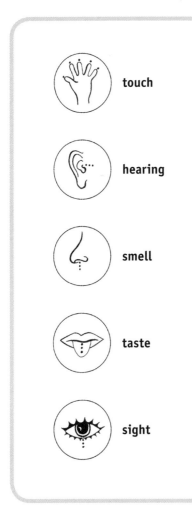 touch

hearing

 smell

 taste

sight

vestibular sense

proprioceptive sense

interoceptive sense

The **hidden senses** operate with receptors *inside* our bodies and are not so commonly known.
- The sense of movement and balance (**vestibular sense**) is located in the inner ear.
- The sense of body position (**proprioceptive sense**) is located in our muscles and joints.

These two senses work closely together to give us information about where our bodies are in space and how to move in a coordinated way.

- The internal organ sense (**interoceptive sense**) is located in our internal organs, i.e. our lungs, bladder, bowels and stomach.

This sense gives us information about what is going on inside our bodies, indicating hunger, a full bladder, feeling hot, experiencing cramps and so on.

Interoception completes the internal picture of our body and works together with the movement and body senses.

 ## Touch (the tactile sense)

*"Touch … is a predominant sense at birth, and probably continues to be more critical to human function throughout life than is generally recognized."* (Jean Ayres)

Touch is the first sense to develop in the womb and one of a baby's most advanced abilities at birth. Newborn babies can feel a whole lot better than they can see, hear or taste. As children develop, their sense of touch grows progressively more accurate. The tactile sense is seated in the skin that has millions of receptors all over our bodies. There are touch receptors inside our mouths, throats and digestive system as well. Receptors (sensory receiving cells) fire up when we are touched or touch someone or something. They then send messages to the spinal cord and brain which in turn will interpret the touch.

> "The tactile sense tells us:
> *This is my body and that is the world."*

## Why the tactile sense is important

Our touch sense is vital in telling us about our body's physical boundary – where it starts, where it ends and where the rest of the world begins. Through the touch sense your child develops an internal map of his body that helps him to interact with the world around him. Your child's early experiences of touch and being touched are essential for survival, understanding the physical world, the development of motor skills, the regulation of mood and emotional wellbeing. Touch stimulation literally keeps us sane! Several studies have shown that early touch, such as skin-to-skin, kangaroo care and daily massage, play a major role in development, as well as positive

**DIFFERENT TOUCH SENSATIONS**

**Light touch** is what it feels like if some-one softly touches you or gently kisses you. It is also the feel of certain clothes on our skin or the feel of grass, sand and soil on our feet or hands. Daily grooming activities such as brushing our teeth and washing our hair and faces provide light touch, as do different food textures. For some children, this type of touch can be distressing and cause sensory overload. Others might not be bothered by it at all.

**Deep pressure** is the sensation pro-vided by strong hugs, massage and heavy blankets. Some children actively seek this type of touch by playing boisterous games, rolling down hills and jumping on trampolines.

**Vibration** is a tactile experience coming from vibrating toys or toothbrushes and appliances such as a washing machine or tumble dryer. Vibration usually has a calming effect, but may irritate some.

**Temperature** is a highly subjective touch experience depending on our unique sensitivity to touch. Some of us love freezing cold drinks or ice cream, while others prefer hot drinks.

**Pain sensations** differ in degrees – from the sting of a vaccination needle to the burn of an open wound when you fall. Some people are very sensi-tive to pain, while others may injure themselves without really noticing. It all depends on your unique threshold.

Each child reacts differently to the various touch sensations – that is what makes him unique.

emotional and mental stability.

Children initially experience touch through holding and cuddling; this helps them to make sense of their world and calms and organises them. Later on they actively seek out touch opportunities, which is fundamental to their physical and emotional development.

The touch sense plays an important role in the development of:

- attachments with people around us
- emotional wellbeing
- body awareness
- motor planning
- language skills
- fine-motor skills
- visual perception skills
- academic learning.

## Touch discrimination

Touch discrimination is the ability to differentiate between various textures, contours and forms by touching them.

Babies and children up to the age of five years feel much more effectively with their mouths than with their hands. They actively use their mouths to explore the shape, size, texture and weight of objects. They learn about soft and hard, smooth and rough, big and small, round and angular, and so on. Babies as young as one month form a mental image of an object by mouthing it. Studies indicate that babies will show a preference for an object that they have mouthed over one that they have never touched. This is very important in terms of linking the senses of touch and sight. The ability to discriminate between different objects using our touch sense is important when we explore the world and learn new movement tasks.

## Everyday touch activities

We are always actively touching, or passively being touched – by other people, clothes, objects, the air on our skin or the ground under our feet. Creating specific touch opportunities for your child has huge benefits.

Encourage textured play so that your child has the opportunity to explore the difference between soft and hard, squashy and sticky, or rough and smooth. Note the texture of the toys and objects that form part of your child's day. If everything is soft and smooth, be intentional and include different textures. Create opportunities for tactile play involving the whole body, not just hands.

### TOUCHY-FEELY TRAVELS

Create a **touchy-feely route** inside your house or outdoors. Use rugs, duvets, sofa cushions, beanbags, pillowcases filled with beans, corrugated cardboard, foam packaging, bubble wrap and anything else that you can think of that adds texture. Encourage your child to walk, crawl, jump or roll from one side of the route to the other over the different textures. Adding a goal is a good way of engaging children who are hesitant. Put puzzle pieces at one side of the road and encourage your child to take one piece at a time to the other side where the picture is waiting, and where the puzzle can be assembled. Play pretend games, for instance follow-my-leader or find the treasure – burying objects such as favourite toy animals, dinosaurs or cars under the duvets and pillows.

### HOT-DOG GAME

Encourage your child to lie on one side of a duvet, a soft blanket, a sleeping bag or foam yoga mat. Roll her up gently yet tightly in the duvet, blanket, sleeping bag or mat until she is like a sausage squeezed in a roll. Depending on how long your child can tolerate this position (some love it and some don't like it that much), move your hands, a therapy ball or a beach ball over her body, from her shoulders all the way to her feet, pretending you are putting some sauce on her. This activity incorporates deep pressure touch, which is calming and organising. It can easily be made part of your morning and/or bedtime routine.

### RUB-A-DUB-DUB

Using a towel, rub your child dry after a bath – first his arms, then his legs and last his tummy and back. This lovely, deep pressure feels good and will calm and organise him.

### BODY MASSAGE

Add massage to your child's routine, even if it is just a few strokes. It could be part of her bedtime routine, or it can be done over weekends or used spontaneously at any time during the day when your child needs some calming touch. Regular massage carries so many benefits – once you are aware of this you will find it difficult not to include it in your child's routine.

### CONTAIN THE MESS OF MESSY PLAY

Touch activities can get messy. For mothers who are hyper neat and slightly OCD about cleaning and cleanliness (I'm one) this can be hard. But developing children aren't meant to stay clean and should not be deprived of textured touch experiences so the house can stay clean. Children who have no or limited opportunities for touch experiences are more likely to become fussy eaters or have difficulty with fine-motor tasks and tasks that require motor planning. Contain the mess by using a small paddling pool (obviously without the water) as the tactile area. Encouraging my children to stay inside this space while making as much mess as they would like, has always worked in my house. Or restrict the mess to a container such as a tray with high sides, plastic sheeting, a high-chair table while your toddler is sitting in the high chair, the bath or a sink.

You can also:

- Set up the sensory play in an area where it is easy to vacuum, mop or wash down, such as the kitchen, in the bath or in the garden.
- Use a Mess Mat or a vinyl tablecloth on the table or on the floor.
- Pour the wet substances into a Ziploc bag and close it securely with some duct tape to prevent it from ripping open. Your child can now explore the texture from the outside of the bag, feeling it move inside. This not only works well for those days when making a mess is not an option; it is also great for children who might be hesitant to touch wet textures. Often seeing the texture and exploring it in this way prepares children for the next step – touching the wet or slimy stuff inside.

### SENSORY BOXES

Sensory boxes for kids provide them with a wonderful opportunity to experience different textures. Fill boxes or plastic containers with a variety of objects that provide texture – smooth or rough, soft or hard, squishy or firm – and encourage your child to play with the contents. This will enhance your child's touch discrimination by allowing her to process different touch sensations. It will also develop creativity, fine-motor skills, motor-planning skills and problem-solving skills. Be creative with your sensory boxes – add anything that is safe and age appropriate: plastic farm animals or dinosaurs, beads of different textures and sizes, spoons and other utensils, pieces of foam rubber, pompoms, balls, cardboard tubes, feathers, elastic bands and bubble wrap. Make several and give each box a theme, for example a nature box including leaves, acorns, pine kernels, stones, seed pods and pieces of wood, or a bathtime box including shaving foam.

Objects and substances used for touch activities should be non-toxic or edible or not harmful. Your toddler might explore by putting things in his mouth, especially with a new activity. Textured touch experiences (dry, wet, slimy and sticky textures) that work well with most kids:

- Colouring rice – colour raw rice by placing it in a Ziploc bag and adding food colouring to it. Give it a good rub and a shake. Mix blue and red food colouring for lavender-coloured rice. Add a few drops of essential oils and the coloured, beautifully scented rice engages not only the sense of touch, but also those of sight and smell.
- Making heaps of dry beans, pasta, lentils and sand.
- Tasting cooked pasta (spaghetti works great, especially when overcooked as it

becomes slightly sticky), custard, jelly, instant pudding mix, whipped cream and yoghurt and rub spoonfuls between the fingers.
- Spreading shaving foam – keep in a container or on the side of the bath – is great, not only for a tactile experience, but also for developing all those little hand and wrist muscles in preparation for writing.
- Corn flour play (my personal favourite) – mix some water with corn flour until it becomes thick – you should still be able to pour it but it should feel solid under pressure.
- Finger painting – make your own by mixing one tablespoon of corn flour, four to six pumps of baby shampoo, a drop of food colouring and one or two teaspoons of water. This can also be used as body paint.

### HIDE-AND-SEEK GAMES
Play hide-and-seek by hiding toys in sand, in play dough, or under a blanket, and letting your child find and identify them with his hands.

---

**TIPS FOR INTENTIONAL PARENTS**
◀ Allow your child to play, get dirty and make a mess without cleaning his hands, face and body immediately.
◀ Although in our western society we teach our children to eat with a spoon, a fork and later use a knife too, we should also provide ample opportunities for them to eat with their hands and give them lots of finger food. This will help them make sense of different textures and other touch properties.
◀ Don't restrict your child's toys to smooth plastic ones. Look for toys with different textures or make your own toys that are furry, rough, squishy, soft, prickly, velvety, bumpy, hard, etc.

---

 # Movement and balance (the vestibular sense)

Movement is the basis of all learning. Children **need to move** in order to learn and develop. The vestibular sense that regulates movement is a highly complex system located inside the ear. It functions twenty-four hours a day. It works together with all the other senses and keeps us awake, calms us down, lets us move and keeps us still – all without us having to think about it.

## Why movement is important

The movement sense works closely with the other senses to make us aware *of where we are in the world* (you could call it your body's *GPS*). The movement sense also helps us to balance and withstand the force of gravity. This is what enables your child to stay upright when she has to sit at the dining room table or on the carpet at story time. It enables her to throw and catch a ball without falling over. Most of the time your child is able to move around, climb up and down, sit and stand without having to consciously think about how to stay upright. It is only when movement becomes quite intense, such as when a child is swinging or jumping high, or when she is thrown up into the air, that she becomes aware of how the movement makes her feel. Some children will complain that it is too much, while others will beg for more.

Our movement system helps us to **regulate**. *Slow, rhythmical movements lower our arousal level*, which is why swinging in a hammock in the garden can send you off to sleep and why we tend to rock our babies in our arms when we want them to go to sleep. *Fast, intense and irregular movements wake us up* – probably the reason why you are not likely to see anyone falling asleep on a rollercoaster. We move all the time – shifting in the chair in an effort to keep awake during a meeting, tapping our foot on the ground to remain calm while waiting for someone who is late, getting up from the desk to make a cup of tea when we feel our concentration drop or chewing gum to focus while we drive. When we are fully engaged in physical activity our brain releases endorphins – those feel-good hormones that **help regulate our mood**. Your happiest childhood memories probably involved movement, whether it is running around chasing a friend, cycling down the street at great speed or being thrown in the air by a playful dad. All of us, children and adults alike, feel better if we move.

> **The brain needs the body to move**
> *There is a perception that we need to sit still to concentrate. Who has not heard (or said) the words: "Sit still and listen!" On the contrary;* **the brain needs the body to move in order to listen**. *The reticular activating system (RAS), an area in the brain that is responsible for keeping us awake and attentive, receives a lot of input from the movement sense. It tells the body to move, because the thinking brain needs movement to wake up. Your child, with his immature brain, needs more movement to stay alert than us grown-ups who have fully developed brains.*

## Everyday movement activities

- Bounce your child on your knees, open your knees and let her fall down backwards while you are holding her hands.
- Let your child ride on your back while you pretend to be a horse. The horse can walk slowly, move quickly, and bounce up and down and sideways, all of which challenges your child's postural control and balancing skills.
- Dance with your child – twirl around, bob up and down, tip him backwards and lift him up.
- Take your child outside in the garden, or to a park, and let her swing, slide, climb up and down, jump on a trampoline, run, tumble and play traditional games like ring o' roses, catch and duck-duck-goose.

- If you are comfortable with it, let you child jump on a bed or a big cushion. When it is raining and you cannot move outside, help your child jump on an exercise ball. Keep the ball in a safe corner with your legs and support your child by holding onto his hips or under his arms while encouraging him to hop, bounce and jump on the ball.
- Place two paper plates on a wooden or tiled surface and let your child place each foot on a separate plate. Tell her to move the paper plates forward, backward and around the room. For the plates to be moved successfully the feet should not be lifted and a certain amount of pressure needs to be applied onto the floor. This is a wonderful activity to get sleepy children from their bedroom to the kitchen in the morning.
- Animal walks are a fun activity and can be done indoors or out. It develops postural muscles, motor planning and sequencing and imagination; the sky is the limit as to the range of walks and animals you can include. Make it part of your morning or bedtime routine, as a means of regulating your child's level of alertness, or simply do it for fun!

    A few examples:
  - Slither like a snake
  - Walk like a crab
  - Wriggle like a worm
  - Jump like a frog
  - Run like a cheetah

**TIPS FOR INTENTIONAL PARENTS**

Movement can be used very successfully to regulate your child.

◀ Use slow, steady movements such as rocking and swinging to calm your child.

◀ Use fast, intense movements such as jumping on a trampoline and crashing into a wall of pillows to energise your child.

◀ Certain movements may cause your child to become dysregulated – either too active or too passive. Examples are spinning and being upside down for too long. You don't have to avoid these movements – you just have to know your child and be aware of how he responds to them. If you are unsure, include a game that involves spinning or being upside down. Avoid overstimulation when playing such games by including stops and starts. For example play a game of "hello/goodbye": spin your child once or twice, stop and say "hello", then spin her the other way and say "goodbye". Stop and start frequently.

**Body position sense (the proprioceptive sense)**

As your baby starts moving – initially through reflexes, then through trial and error and later more purposefully – she learns about her own body and how it relates to the world and the space around her. Each time she moves a muscle the body sense receptors are switched on. They enable her to form an *internal map of her body,* which later becomes intuitive – to the point where she knows what her body looks and feels like even when she sleeps. In short, the proprioceptive sense is the one that tells us: *"This is where I am and this is what I'm doing."* It provides information not only about our body's position, but also about the intricate qualities of the space in which we are moving.

## Why the proprioceptive system is important

An amazing fact about the proprioceptive system is that we are almost completely unaware of it when it is at work. It is only really when we are learning a new skill that we are vaguely aware of this system. Every single motor task requires the activation of and feedback from this system. Getting out of bed in the morning requires the proprioceptive system to give you information about how you need to lift off the duvet, how to swing your legs to the side of the bed, and how much force you need to move into a sitting and then a standing position. Staying put while sleeping also needs this system to work. The reason why young children might fall off the first few nights when they are moved from a cot to a "big bed" is that there are no longer bed rails to provide the physical boundary that learning bodies and brains need.

The proprioceptive sense is the first system that is affected when we are exhausted and stressed. Tired children become clumsy and accident prone, so a late night often ends with at least one child getting hurt and bursting into tears. I know I'm really tired when I drop objects or something ends up being broken while I'm unpacking the dishwasher (something I do every single day).

Do you remember when your toddler learnt to walk up stairs? Not only did she look down at her legs and feet, she would also lift her leg up way too high before plonking it down on the next step. When young children learn how to ride a bike, they either push down too hard or not hard enough on the pedals. So they may lose their balance, or have difficulty propelling the bike forward. Through the feedback they receive from their proprioceptive system, they **learn how to judge the force, direction, position and speed of their movements,** so that tasks like walking, climbing stairs and riding a bike become more coordinated, less clumsy and more efficient.

When we know where our bodies are and how to move purposefully, we feel safe and secure. When we trust our own bodies, we are able to challenge them by trying new and unfamiliar tasks and perfecting familiar tasks. The proprioceptive sense is **the greatest organiser and regulator** of all the senses. Proprioception is what makes us feel good – organised, calm and attentive – ready to learn and interact with the world and people.

When things are out of sync and out of balance, the proprioceptive system helps to bring harmony and get our bodies and brains in sync.

- When we are down, drowsy or inattentive, it can energise us and focus our attention.
- When we are overloaded, stressed and out of control, it can contain us and decrease the anxiety.

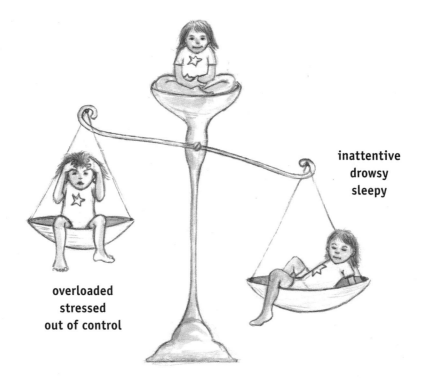

inattentive
drowsy
sleepy

overloaded
stressed
out of control

What do you do to get rid of stress when you feel exhausted and tense? Do you go for a run or a ride on your bike, have a long warm bath, drink a glass of wine or chew gum? Most of the activities that make us feel better involve some form of calming movement and deep pressure touch.

**TIPS FOR INTENTIONAL PARENTS**

Children *always* benefit from proprioceptive input – it will support them in feeling calm, alert and ready to learn. If your child's body is like an engine that requires fuel to get it going and keeps it going, then proprioceptive input is that fuel. A little bit at a time spread throughout the day keeps the engine running at just the right level – never in danger of running on empty, or of flooding. So this is the goal: *make proprioceptive input part of your child's daily routine.* Let him walk like a crab to the bathroom, suck yoghurt through a straw at breakfast, carry a fairly heavy backpack to the car, eat crunchy snacks throughout the day and have fun playing rough and tumble with dad before bathtime.

At times your child may seem lethargic, sluggish and slow to get going and keep going, but at other times he may seem to bounce off the wall. Both states will affect his ability to attend to the task at hand and stay focused. This is when the proprioceptive system needs to be activated through movement to get him out of the danger zone.

## Everyday activities for proprioception

Proprioceptors located in the muscles, joints and tendons are activated when your body moves; especially if the movement is against gravity – movement that makes your body work hard. The types of movements to be encouraged are **pulling, pushing, crashing and lifting** – anything that gets the deep muscles going. Unfortunately, in our modern society characterised by city living, we don't get many routine opportunities for heavy work.

   Children living in rural areas routinely do more pulling, pushing and lifting throughout the day. They walk or cycle from place to place, whereas city dwellers would be driven by car or bus. Many of these activities are goal-directed, which generally have a regulating and calming effect. Carrying buckets of water home from the nearest water source, fetching wood and helping with domestic cleaning and caring for animals, are examples how proprioception happens naturally. As a child I had to cycle to school and extra-mural activities; a heavy backpack on my back and even a bulky Spanish flamenco skirt hanging over the handlebars. But today, because of safety concerns and all sorts of other reasons, many children are driven by car wherever they need to go. Herein lies your challenge – you have to "invent" opportunities for heavy work, be creative and find ways of including them into your child's day. This is one of the most valuable secrets to ensure that our children stay happy, connected and well regulated.

### FUN GAMES – INSIDE AND OUTSIDE
- Jungle gyms offer great opportunities for proprioceptive input, e.g. climbing up using the rope or the ladder, attempting monkey bars, hanging on a rope.
- Jumping on a small or large trampoline is great for proprioception. A small trampoline inside the house is perfect for rainy or cold weather. Most days before school, come rain or shine, I encourage my girls to jump on an exercise ball, which I squeeze in a corner and support with my legs. We jump to the beat of a song, we do our ABCs, we count and we make up funny rhymes.
- Find a safe, carpeted spot to build a tower of soft bedding, pillows and cushions. Kids will have great fun and get lots of proprioceptive input by running and crashing into the pile.
- Ride a tricycle or bicycle or push a push-bike.
- Play with play dough.
- Knead dough for bread or biscuits, or make mud pies.
- Animal movements: jump like a frog; walk on all fours like a bear.
- Carry heavy items such as buckets filled with sand or water, or bags of groceries from the car.
- Wheelbarrow walking.
- Blow on a kazoo, whistle or other noise maker.
- Play blow-football (blowing a cotton ball through straws).

### MEAL-TIMES
- Suck yoghurt, a smoothie or jelly through a long, twisty straw.
- Eat crunchy foods, such as apples, raw carrots and peppers, nuts and seeds.

**BATHTIME FUN**
- Squirt water out of spray bottles.
- Blow bubbles through a straw.
- Dunk sponges with different sizes and shapes into the water and squeeze the water out.

**ROUGH-AND-TUMBLE PLAY (MY PERSONAL FAVOURITE)**
Baby animals spend a lot of time engaged in physical play with their siblings. They wrestle, hold on to and crawl over one another. They romp around, nibbling at one another's ears, tails and paws. They make balletic movements with their spines curved or jump gracefully into the air.

Rough-and-tumble play is a great medium for social, emotional and physical development in children. It is also my favourite because there is nothing quite like it to teach children about self-regulation. It helps them get rid of aggression and frustration, develops confidence, builds relationships and is excellent for physical development.

# Smell (the olfactory sense) and taste (the gustatory sense)

Smells, emotions and memory go hand-in-hand. Smell is a unique sense; the information we receive from receptors in our nose is transmitted directly to the emotional and memory centres in the brain. This explains the strong memories and feelings evoked by a certain smell, such as the smell of biscuits baking that takes you back to your granny's home and holidays spent in her kitchen. Smell cells die as a result of infections and exposure to pollutants and toxins, and are replaced about once every two months. They degenerate over time and our sense of smell declines as we age; this is why your toddler often notices and points out smells that you haven't even been aware of.

## Why smelling and tasting are important

Smell and taste, which are chemical senses, are intertwined. About seventy-five per cent of what we taste is actually what we smell. Our senses of smell and taste are vital for **survival** and to keep us **safe**. They are also important in the **bonding** process, creating **emotional security** and building **memories**.

Babies rely heavily on their sense of smell for feeding – when they smell the familiarity of their mother's breast, their uncoordinated body movements slow down and they become calm and regulated. The sense of smell plays a vital role in establishing mother-infant bonding.

The sense of taste starts developing in the third trimester of pregnancy, is quite well developed at birth, and plays an important role in growth. We are programmed to like sweet and salty tastes, and food preferences are built on experience. A bitter taste may indicate that something could be dangerous. Certain foods – sweets and fats – have mood-altering effects and can calm a child, improve his attention span or help him sleep.

As adults, we can go for days without even noticing smells, so it may be difficult for us to recognise how different smells can affect the behaviour of our children. When my husband goes away on business trips, our daughters miss him terribly. One of my girls then takes one of his T-shirts and holds it close to her face and says, "I like the smell of Daddy". This illustrates how effective the sense of smell is in calming and regulating. On the other hand, the sense of smell can cause real dysregulation in some kids. My youngest daughter complains terribly if we go into smelly public toilets or when she has to sit through a family dinner including food with a distinct smell. Recently she said: "Mm, if you can get past the smell, it actually doesn't taste too bad." We've come a long way for her to at least try the "awful smelling" food without kicking up a fuss!

## The effect of specific smells

Certain smells will have a calming effect, while others will have an energising effect.

| Smells that calm and relax | Smells that alert and energise |
|:---:|:---:|
| Lavender | Peppermint |
| Camomile | Basil |
| Rose | Lemon |
| | Cinnamon |
| | Rosemary |

## Fun games involving the sense of smell

- Add aromatherapy oils to home-made play dough. Which oil will depend on the effect that you want it to have on your child. Playing with lavender dough after dinnertime will calm your child and set the scene for the bedtime routine. Playing with lemon-scented dough on the way to school will energise him.
- Home-made scented lotions can be used in the same way.
- Use scratch-and-smell stickers and scented felt-tip pens to achieve a specific effect.

**TIP FOR INTENTIONAL PARENTS**
Be mindful that strong perfumes and pungent smells might cause your child to behave in uncharacteristic ways. You might not even notice a smell but your child's nose and taste buds are far more sensitive than yours.

## Sight (the visual sense)

The visual sense is the only sense that receives no stimulation in the womb; as a result this sense is the least developed at birth. A child's sight develops rapidly until the age of two. The process then slows down but continues until the child is eight or nine.

## Why the visual sense is important

It is through our eyes that we are able to take in the most information from our environment. Sight allows us to move in relation to what we see, such as when we have to catch a ball, drive a car or write on a line. It works very closely with the senses of touch, movement, proprioception and hearing. Vision develops quickly and goes on to dominate the human sensory experience – even more so in this age where everything is visual.

   The visual sense involves far more than simply seeing. Everybody knows the expression "A picture is worth a thousand words"; a complex idea can be conveyed with a single still image. Vision is what we rely on to understand what we see, and then to coordinate what we see with the information from other senses.

   **Your child uses his visual system, not only to see, but also to**
- move
- think
- relate.

*Visual thinking is essential for learning*. As your child develops he acquires the ability to transfer a visual image and idea into his play. Your little girl who is pretending to be a fairy and "flies" around, waving her arms up and down, and your little boy pretending to be a pirate sailing on his ship when he is playing on your couch, are able to visualise what fairies or pirates look like and how they move. The development of this vital skill starts when your baby learns to associate visual images with words. Visual information tells the mind how to think and the body how to move.

## Hearing (the auditory sense)

The auditory sense is constantly active, even during sleep, and impacts on all aspects of everyday functioning. It is closely connected with the touch, movement and visual senses, and provides your child with a "map" of his body and his environment. The sense of hearing develops in the womb and matures gradually until your child reaches school-going age. It is absolutely essential for the development of his language skills. Your toddler can hear high-tone frequencies better than you, which could explain why he is sensitive to the sounds of the hand-dryer in public toilets and a whistling kettle. His ability to discriminate sounds in a noisy setting, such as you calling him when he's outside playing, doesn't fully mature until the age of about ten. And these days we are competing with traffic, television and electronic toys when trying to communicate with our kids – no wonder we often have to call them at least three times before they respond! (When this happens, don't assume that your child is being disobedient. Chances are that he simply isn't able to distinguish your voice from all the other sounds around him.)

Ear infections affect children's hearing and may hamper language development. Most children will suffer from a bout or two of infections between six months and three years. Recurring acute infections – more than three times in five months – can hamper auditory discrimination and may result in the loss of the ability to hear very high frequencies.

## Why hearing is important

- Through hearing, children experience language and music, both of which are important for intellectual development.
- Hearing is also vital for emotional development, allowing communication between parents and children, helping them form bonds and strong attachments.

**TIP FOR INTENTIONAL PARENTS**
Pay attention to the sounds in your house and when you are out and about. Children are much better off listening to one thing at a time than having to deal with lots of background noises, such as music blaring in the kitchen competing with the TV in the lounge while the adults are having a conversation – all at the same time. Turn off the TV if you're not actively watching.

## Internal organ sense (the interoceptive sense)

This sense is responsible for letting us know that it is hot, that our bladder is full, that we are hungry and that we need to do something about it. Just like with all the other senses, the way that our children process information from this sense will help us to understand their behaviour. I've had so many questions over the years from mothers who have had difficulty potty training their toddlers, or who wonder why their children never seem to feel hot or cold or hungry or thirsty. When information from the interoceptive sense is not processed adequately, it will result in a child who is either under-responsive or one who is over-responsive to the information. This can account for difficulties with potty training, mood swings and poor regulation of basic needs such as hunger, thirst and body temperature.

# Sensory Processing:
# When body and brain come together

The senses receive all the information we need to function: the five commonly known senses give us information about what is going on around us and the three hidden senses provide information about what is happening inside our bodies. But what happens next? We see something, but what is it? We feel something but what do we do with it? This is where the nervous system, consisting of 100 billion neurons, the spinal cord and the brain, come in. Our brain acts like the CEO of our body, making decisions about *what to do* with the information (should I use it or should I lose it?) and *how to use it* (give meaning to it). Only then can we act appropriately. For the most part, this process happens automatically – without us being consciously aware of how hard our brains are working. No wonder I need my seven hours of sleep at night!

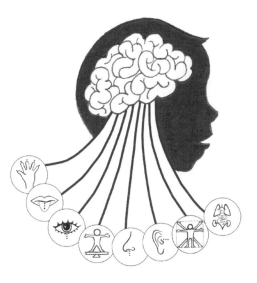

## Sensory modulation: the balancing act of the brain

Your brain acts like a specialised thermostat – it strives to maintain a middle ground, a comfort zone, that "just right" place in which you feel comfortable to interact with the world and the people within. The more time we spend in this place, the happier we feel. We feel more connected and less stressed. This thermostat needs to filter information: *ignoring familiar and irrelevant information*, while *paying attention to important and meaningful information*. Your brain is constantly working at a complex balancing act of ignoring and paying attention. This process makes it possible for you to read this book while ignoring background noises like the air-conditioner and the label in your shirt that may be a bit scratchy. No wonder there are days when we feel totally exhausted. In this busy, noisy and demanding world in which we live, balancing it all obviously requires a huge effort from our brains.

Everyone's brain is **wired in a unique way, each with a unique thermostat**. Some of us love the hustle and bustle of this sensory-rich world, enjoying busy shopping malls, thrilling rollercoaster rides, hot spicy food and loud music. Others prefer a world where less is more: a cosy corner in a restaurant, going to Pilates and walking in the mountains. And it's okay – we can't all be the same. In fact, it is great, because each of us was created for a unique and very specific purpose.

*To explain this important concept, the analogy of a fuel tank might be useful. Different types of cars have different sizes of fuel tanks – small, medium or large. Likewise our brains and that of our children are biologically wired to have a **small, medium or large fuel tank**.*

*Some children have a small tank that fills up quickly – their brain seems more sensitive and requires less input filling it up. With a small tank, at times it seems as if the tank overflows, which might manifest in a meltdown, anxiety or aggression. These children remind me of **hedgehogs** – small animals who don't need a lot of food. When things get too much, they curl up into a ball with their quills extended to protect themselves.*

*Other children have large tanks that need more fuel to fill up – their brain seems less sensitive and requires large amounts of input to fill them up. When their tanks aren't full, they might seem unaware of their surroundings, in dreamland and slow to respond. These children remind me of **giraffes** – large animals that need large amounts of food. With their long neck and legs they move slowly and are slower to get going.*

*Then there are children who have even bigger fuel tanks with engines that guzzle fuel – no matter how much we fill up their tanks, before they know it, it's empty. They end up craving more input – often movement and touch – which means that they are active, always on the go and seeking variety. These children remind me of **monkeys** – active and always looking for more.*

# Factors influencing sensory processing

Sensory processing is not static – it depends not only on our unique temperament, it is also influenced by other factors.

## Time of day

Early morning and late afternoons are often the most challenging, as these are times when our ability to filter sensations is hugely affected by our biological needs – hunger and fatigue. At the end of a long day, our brains have been bombarded with sensory input and have had to work extensively to process all of this information. At this time of day it will be difficult for even the most laid-back child and parent to stay calm and patient.

## Setting

I often hear mums say to teachers, "Surely the child you are describing is not my child?" Our children often respond differently when they are not in their familiar home environment or with their primary caregivers. Looking at the situation in which the child finds himself at any given time helps us understand and appreciate why the same child may be easy-going in one environment but shy or slow to warm up in another.

## Age

During the first few months of life, babies learn how to self-regulate with your help. They learn how to stay calm while becoming interested in and deriving pleasure from the sights, sounds, tastes and touch sensations in their world. As your baby develops, the filtering system in his brain matures, age becomes less significant and he learns how to stay calm and self-regulate.

## Stress

Neuro-scientific research has proved that, contrary to popular belief, children do experience stress. Every time a child is introduced to something new, a low-level stress response is activated; the ways in which they respond to this differ hugely and are unique to each child. Your youngest will most likely not respond in the same way when he starts nursery school than your eldest when he was left without you for the first time. The stress hormones, cortisol and adrenaline, cause changes in the way the brain functions. When we are extremely stressed, the brain goes into overdrive and a child who is usually easy-going might become fractious, overactive or even aggressive. The same applies to you – you might be able to deal with the demands of your toddler when you are calm and well rested but – oh dear – when you are stressed and tired, the same little toddler with the same demands could cause you to lose your temper.

Our brains are amazing, processing information every nano-second of the day, without us being consciously aware of it. "*Over 80 percent of the nervous system is involved in processing or organizing sensory input, and thus the brain is primarily a sensory processing machine.*" Jean Ayres.

# Your child's developing brain

*"Rabbit's clever," said Pooh thoughtfully.*

*"Yes," said Piglet, "Rabbit's clever."*

*"And he has Brain."*

*"Yes," said Piglet, "Rabbit has Brain."*

*There was a long silence.*

*"I suppose," said Pooh, "that that's why he never understands anything."*

– A.A. Milne, *Winnie-the-Pooh*

Your toddler is experiencing an explosive rush of brain development; understanding a little bit of what is happening inside his brain and how it affects his behaviour, will help you feel more in control. You'll be able to understand him better, respond more effectively to challenging behaviour and work towards forming a strong relationship.

In this chapter we will take a short journey into your child's amazing brain. We will discuss:

- What your child's brain looks like – three main parts and two hemispheres;
- How and when your child's brain matures; and
- Five ingredients for a healthy brain.

I am fascinated with child development. To observe and experience first-hand how children develop, has been a hobby, a passion and a job (as mum and therapist). From that tiny little bundle who grabs the toy, the crawling baby who is actively exploring every corner of the house, to the young toddler who takes his first wobbly steps. The first sounds, the babbling, then words and finally sentences – every little milestone a celebration. I'm in awe of their little bodies and ever changing developing brains.

Being a parent certainly doesn't require you to have an interest in neuroscience and brain development. However, I believe that knowing a little will change a lot.

Knowing the following will be life-changing for you and your child:
- your toddler's brain is immature;
- his immature brain leads him to behave in certain ways;
- significant changes happen while your child is growing up; and
- how you parent will affect how your child's brain is wired.

## Parenting and your child's brain

Years and years of neuroscience, brain scans and research have provided us with vital information about how our children's brains develop and mature. We now know that, although genes play a major role in brain development, our parenting, coupled with the opportunities we give our children, have a dramatic effect on how our children's brains are shaped. It is the interplay between *nature* (genes) and *nurture* (you and the environment) that shapes our children's brains. Although we have little influence over the genetic make-up, the hardwiring with which our children come into this world, the nurture part, our parenting, is something we should not underestimate. By being intentional about how we parent we can have a massive impact on our children's lives – helping them understand their own unique temperament and how to feel, think and behave.

## The maturing brain

Brain maturation will result in whole-brain functioning and the emergence of self-regulation skills – as soon as the thinking part of your child's brain kicks in, she will start to develop the ability to calm herself, control her impulses and deal with big feelings, such as anger, frustration and disappointment. While your child's brain is in the process of maturing – making important connections – she needs *you*. She needs a connection with you that encompasses empathy, understanding, warmth and attentiveness.

## Unfinished business

When my children were little, I often felt frustrated because I never seemed able to start and finish a time-consuming task, such as sorting out their playroom cupboard, in one go. I'd put them to bed for an afternoon nap and get started. But, mark my words, on the day that I really bargained on them napping for the whole 2 hours, they would wake up at just the moment when all the toys were lying on the floor (not merely lying on the floor, but meticulously grouped according to a specific categorising system of which only I knew the formula). There was nothing I could do but wait until the next nap time before finishing the task. To my frustration, it took more than a few nap times before that cupboard was finally done.

The same applies to your child's brain. It takes time, lots of time (and patience on our side) to develop. Our children don't wake up one morning able to control their impulses, reason maturely and make deliberate decisions leading to increased productivity. Their brains are constantly developing; in fact, research has discovered that even teenagers' brains continue to develop, and our brains aren't considered fully developed until we reach our mid-twenties. Brain development in the young child is truly unfinished business.

That is the *bad news*: you will have to wait for your child's brain to develop. It will take time. So unless you understand some of the fundamental concepts about brain development, the danger is that you might get trapped in feelings of frustration or bewilderment when you expect either too much or too little from your child.

The *good news* is: your child's brain will change in response to your parenting. No pressure! There is no doubt that how we parent matters enormously. But don't get stressed out and try to make every moment count. Don't feel guilty about the times when you perhaps didn't use opportunities to parent perfectly.

Remember: there is no such thing as perfect parenting or the perfect parent. It is all about acknowledging our vulnerability, being conscious, deliberate, mindful and *intentional*. You will not get it right each and every time. Intentional parenting is about one important fundamental principle that in itself will change how your child's brain is wired: *your relationship with your child*.

> "When we understand our children's unique temperament and how to parent their developing brains we can connect with our children in deep and meaningful ways."

# What the brain looks like

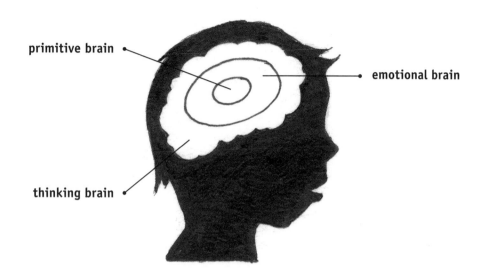

Your child's brain consists of three main parts:
- The primitive brain (the brain stem and cerebellum)
- The emotional brain (the limbic system)
- The thinking brain (the cortex and frontal lobes)

## The primitive brain

This is the deepest part of the brain and guides behaviour vital for survival. It is the control centre for all the functions that keep us alive without being consciously aware of how hard it is working. It includes the regulation of:

- Breathing
- Circulation
- Temperature
- Hunger (informing you when you need to eat and when you are full)
- Movement, posture and balance
- Stress response (fight or flight)

## The emotional brain

This part of the brain forms the bridge between the lower primitive part and the higher thinking part. This part of the brain enables us to give meaning to what we see, hear, smell, taste and feel. We attach emotions to sensations. It also helps control the stress response (fight or flight): *Is what I'm feeling good or is it dangerous?* This part of the brain triggers strong emotions such as:

- Fear
- Rage
- Distress
- Love
- Ecstasy

## The thinking brain

The frontal part, or the higher brain, is the biggest and most sophisticated part of the brain. It acts as the CEO of the brain, consciously managing our intentions, emotions and behaviours by drawing from previous experiences and problem-solving. Your parenting has a massive impact on this part of your child's brain. The thinking brain develops over time and forms strong connections that regulate complex skills such as:

- Controlling our body and our emotions
- Focus, attention and self-discipline
- Creativity, imagination and flexibility
- Problem-solving and decision-making
- Reasoning and reflection
- Self-awareness and self-confidence
- Kindness, empathy and caring

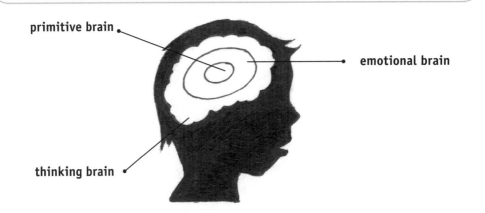

# The two sides

The brain has two sides (two hemispheres), connected by a bundle of fibres called the *corpus callosum*.

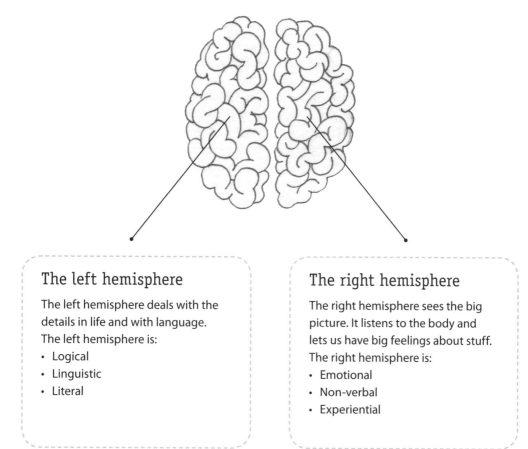

## The left hemisphere

The left hemisphere deals with the details in life and with language. The left hemisphere is:

- Logical
- Linguistic
- Literal

## The right hemisphere

The right hemisphere sees the big picture. It listens to the body and lets us have big feelings about stuff. The right hemisphere is:

- Emotional
- Non-verbal
- Experiential

**The brain (in a nutshell):**
- We need our senses to feed into the *primitive* brain in order for us to survive and make sense of the world.
- We need the *emotional* brain to attach meaning and memory to sensations.
- We need our *thinking brain* to solve problems and make good decisions.
- We need the *left* brain to give words and logic to the overwhelming emotions we experience in the *right* brain.

# How it develops

## Thinking brain under construction

At birth your baby's brain is about a quarter of its eventual size. It is like a house that's being built. It is not yet completed. For the young child, this means that their primitive and emotional brains are in the driving seat. What they feel, see and hear drives their behaviour and their emotions, which explains why toddlers have lots of *big emotions* that lead to distress, tantrums, meltdowns, kicking and screaming. **When a toddler gets upset, the thinking brain, which controls language and logic, shuts down. Their primitive brain is in the driving seat.** In fact, that is exactly what happens in our adult brains too: if I get angry, stressed and upset, I have to work very hard at controlling my language and thoughts because my primitive brain is taking over in a big way! And herein lies the difference: your child's brain has not yet fully established the critical connections necessary for the thinking brain to help with the regulation of the primitive brain. Toddlers fall apart because their brains can't keep it together … yet.

> Maia has been awake for well over an hour and her body is craving food. Her primitive brain is in the driving seat. "Maia, breakfast is ready", comes the call from the kitchen. Maia is making a secret diary. She is very involved and focused and when Mum calls she actually gets a fright. Now her primitive brain is not only craving food, it is also in a state of alarm. It's all guns blazing: with her primitive brain in the driving seat, she finds it difficult to deal with feelings of frustration, to control her impulses and to do some problem solving. She screams, "No!" and throws herself on the floor in tears.

As your child grows and develops, connections form across different parts of the brain, enabling the brain to function as a whole. The connections consolidate over time laying the foundations for success later in life. One of our goals as parents is to help our children build strong connections between the upper and lower brain, so that the two can work as a team. Only then will they be able to experience big feelings (such as joy, excitement, frustration and anger), and have the courage to acknowledge and move through them without either shutting them off or going off the rails. Like a winning rugby team needs all fifteen players, each with an allocated position, working together to achieve one goal, so we need the different areas of our brain to work together. Your child's every experience will create connections in his highly adaptable brain. Think of the brain as a muscle – the more we exercise it, the stronger it gets.

Let's return to Maia's meltdown. How would a warm, attentive mother support her child in developing the strong brain connections required for healthy development?

Maia's mum realises what is happening and thinks of ways in which to help Maia through this meltdown (a period of dysregulation). She knows that there will be no eating, no negotiating, no problem-solving and no restoration of calm unless Maia is able to move through the period of dysregulation. She **connects with Maia** by saying, "I'm sorry, did I give you a fright calling you from downstairs? It must be difficult for you to stop working on your special book." Maia's mother is acknowledging her feelings and giving her some words to help her make sense of them.

Then Mum gives her some **calming sensory input**. She puts Maia on her lap and gives her a firm, deep hug because deep pressure touch restores calm.

Next she **activates Maia's thinking brain** by saying, "I've heard your baby crying; perhaps she also needs some breakfast. Let's fetch her so that we can feed her too." She is using distraction to get the thinking brain going and change Maia's primitive state of behaviour.

Your child's brain develops as he grows. His brain is shaped by experiences and rich, meaningful relationships – especially the connection with you.

Whole-brain function doesn't happen overnight and it is important that we realise this so that:
- We don't have unrealistic expectations of the behaviour our children are capable of; and
- We are intentional in how we interact with our children and what experiences we expose them to.

# Five ingredients for developing a healthy brain

Your child comes into this world with genes providing a base for his brain to develop. But how strong your child's brain becomes and how well his brain will work as a whole depends on some basic factors, which include the way that you parent. A healthy brain needs these five ingredients to develop:
- Movement
- Sleep
- A healthy diet
- Motivation
- Warm, attentive and intentional parenting

## Movement

Movement is one of the key components underlying all development. It wires up the brain. When children move their bodies, the movement releases feel-good hormones and positive proteins that are important for healthy brain development. It has been reported in research that even 5–10 minutes of an activity that involves the whole body in heavy muscle and joint movement, can have an effect lasting up to 2 hours. Your toddler's day should be dotted with movement activities.

## Sleep

Enough sleep is vital for a child's brain to develop optimally. Quality and quantity is important:
- Children between 1 and 3 years need 12–14 hours' sleep a night.
- Children between 3 and 5 years need 11–13 hours' sleep a night.
- Children between 5 and 12 years need 10–11 hours' sleep a night.

See page 101 for more information on healthy sleep.

## A healthy diet

Between the ages of three and ten a child's brain consumes twice as much glucose than that of an adult. During this phase his brain is in the business of forming a vast number of new connections. A healthy diet, consisting of fruits, vegetables, complex carbohydrates, healthy fats and protein provided at the right times of day (at least three meals with two snacks in between), is vital for healthy brain development in children. Food plays a role in improving concentration and energy levels. Irritability and mood swings often result in the primitive brain taking over and may lead to meltdowns. This will be reduced with a healthy diet.
- Omega-3 fatty acids are the essential building blocks of a healthy brain – these are found in fruits, vegetables, nuts and fish.
- *When* our children eat, is as important as *what* they are eating. They should never skip breakfast, as this is the fuel that gets the brain fired up. Eating breakfast helps children learn and develop, and it helps to prevent challenging behaviour. Protein wakes us up and complex carbohydrates provide the fuel that keeps us going, e.g. oats with fruit and nuts, or a slice of whole-wheat toast with a boiled egg. (See page 145 for more information on a healthy diet.)

## Motivation and having fun

Think of the brain as a muscle; with training it keeps in shape, it develops and grows strong. Athletes who train the same muscles over and over usually end up with some muscles overdeveloped and others underdeveloped, which may result in injuries. The same happens in the brain. If you perform the same familiar activities over and over, no new brain connections or pathways will form. You need to engage in new, unfamiliar activities that will result in the formation of new connections and pathways.

Motivation is at the heart of all goal-directed behaviour, and many parts of the brain will become involved in a task if we are motivated to do it. Imagine a toddler seeing an interesting object on the mantelpiece. His motivation to get to it sets everything in motion: his senses work together to get his body organised, plan his movements and negotiate the space in which his body has to move for him to climb onto the couch and reach for the object. How is this significant? If your child is motivated to do something and engaged or focused while doing it, his brain will continue to form new pathways and enable him to develop various skills.

This principle can be applied to encourage children to do jobs around the house. They generally don't like tidying up, taking their plates to the kitchen, making their beds or brushing their teeth. For us, these activities have become automatic – they don't require the same amount of motor control, planning, organising and sequencing as they do for children. Once complex motor tasks are done routinely, they become automatic and hard-wired, and we can do them without thinking: like riding a bike, brushing our teeth and unpacking a dishwasher. Making such routine tasks fun and pleasurable will switch on your child's emotional brain, get the positive hormones flowing and help her to enjoy what she is doing (with less moaning and groaning). Children develop best if we can get them engaged and motivated. Having fun is a key element.

# Warm, attentive and intentional parenting

Every time you interact with your child, her brain forms connections between brain cells and, as time goes by and interaction becomes more complex, the connections between the lower brain and the higher brain are forged. We should enjoy playing and having fun with our kids and help them when they are overwhelmed and have to deal with *big feelings* such as rage, fear, separation, distress and even joy. Aim to connect in good *and* difficult times. Margot Sunderland says, "With emotionally responsive parenting, vital connections will form in [the child's] brain, enabling him to cope well with stress in later life, form fulfilling relationships, manage anger well, be kind and compassionate, have the will and motivation to follow his ambitions and his dreams, experience the deepest calm, and be able to love intimately and in peace." This is quite a mouthful – really a good description of what I want for my children.

## Connecting with your child

Women experience the birth of their baby as an intensely emotional event. But that doesn't mean every woman automatically and instantly falls in love with the baby there and then. Many certainly do, but for others the intense love for their baby comes a little later – and that's okay. And, even if you did feel that you had formed that strong bond with your baby, there might be times during your child's life when you feel less connected. It is not always easy to stay in love with a toddler with whom you can't seem to reason, who won't take "no" for an answer and who won't share anything with anybody. But we have to remember that, as parents, we should be the well from which our children are able to refill their cups when necessary. When they are hungry, tired, lonely or hurt, we should be there to provide food, warmth, loving physical contact and soothing. We should also be there to share in their moments of joy and excitement.

## Reconnecting during trying times

Physical touch, including hugs, cuddles and rough-and-tumble play, releases the feel-good hormones (oxytocin and opioids) that strengthen the bond between people and reduce levels of anxiety and stress. If you feel that it is difficult to connect with your child, try some of the following:

- Hold her close, cuddle up and tell or read her a story or sing a favourite song.
- Be playful and engage in rough and tumble, e.g. throw your child up in the air, hold him tightly and roll with him, let him sit on your knees and play horsey-horsey, swing him around by his hands or turn him upside down and swing him by his feet.
- Play peek-a-boo and hide-and-seek games (this works with babies, toddlers and even pre-schoolers); throw a scarf or blanket over your face, hide behind obstacles such as furniture and build up the anticipation and excitement).
- Massage your child or rub her down firmly with a towel after a bath, shower or swim.
- Roll him up in a blanket and play the hot-dog game (see page 19).
- Give her pillow hugs (place a pillow between you and your child and then hug her – especially useful if your child shies away from direct contact with you).
- Play games with lots of face-to-face interactions, such as putting stickers on each other's noses, cheeks and foreheads. Pull funny faces at each other. Play a staring game and see who laughs first.
- Shower your child with comforting words, loving smiles and laughter. Re-establish connection by focusing on the positive attributes in your child and pointing these out to him. Good affirmations are short, specific to the child and the situation and used daily. Examples of affirmations:
  "You are good at drawing."
  "You are really trying hard."
  "You are so helpful."
  "You are a good friend because you share your toys."
  "You are kind."
  "You are great at solving problems."
  "You are great at finding ways of doing tricky things."
  "You are loved."
  "You can do it!"
  "You are brave."
  "You are special."
  "I believe in you."
  "I will always be here for you."
  "I am proud of you."
  "I love you."

**BOYS AND THEIR BIKES; GIRLS AND THEIR DOLLS**

There are subtle differences in the development of boys' and girls' brains, owing to genes, hormones, environments and experience. Generally speaking, the oestrogen that girls have in their bodies actually increases the rate of brain growth, which means that they are ahead of boys throughout childhood. Boys have slightly larger brains and the average boy tends to be better at visual-spatial tasks. Girls are slightly more advanced at verbal skills and reading non-verbal cues in another person's face.

Boys typically tend to gravitate towards playing with guns, swords and anything that moves or has wheels. This type of play supports their genetically hard-wired brain development, which is enhanced in the area of visual-spatial skill development. By contrast, girls will typically further reinforce their verbal and social skills by playing "mummy-and-baby" games with dolls or siblings. Owing to the plasticity of the brain (the fact that areas not being hard-wired for function are able to develop), parents can provide opportunities for boys and girls to encourage the development of the areas they tend to neglect slightly. Boys will benefit from a mum or dad who engages in lots of conversations while playing. They are good at making "Aahhh", "Uurrgghhh" and "Phewww"" sounds while they are playing, but they often don't provide any more information. Asking *why, how, when* questions will engage the higher parts of their brains and develop their verbal and problem-solving skills, as well as increase self-control. Girls, on the other hand, will benefit from doing jigsaw puzzles and block-building, and Lego should be on every birthday list, as these activities will enhance their visual-spatial skills.

# Your child's unique sensory temperament

························································

*"The things that make me different are the things that make me."*

– A.A. Milne, *Winnie-the-Pooh*

Some children are social, alert and on the move, others are laid-back, easy and adjustable, while others are sensitive, attentive and thoughtful. Your child is born with a unique temperament – a combination of qualities inherited from her parents and shaped by the environment in which she grows up (which includes how she is parented). Don't take it for granted that your little toddler will be a thrill-seeking adrenaline-junkie just like his dad. He might end up being more like you, a slightly more sensitive bookworm. Or he might end up being a little bit of both.

When you understand your child's sensory temperament, his true nature, you will be able to connect with him, tune in to his needs and manage challenges along the way.

In this chapter we will look at the three different sensory temperaments and you will discover which temperament best describes your child.

- The monkey – social, alert and on the move
- The hedgehog – sensitive, attentive and thoughtful
- The giraffe – laid-back, easy-going and adaptable

We will discuss the advantages, disadvantages and challenges of each temperament. I guarantee that reading this chapter will produce lots of "aha moments".

# Each child is unique

I love watching children. What they do and say, how they interact with this world, fascinate me. When my first-born was a baby, she used to love being swaddled and gently rocked before I put her down to sleep. Along came my second baby and, although she also loved being tightly wrapped, she wanted to be put down straight away and fall asleep independently. All children behave in a way that is unique to them, even children with the same gene pool, from the same mum and dad, growing up in the same environment.

In the early 1970s Dr T. Berry Brazelton spent years observing infant behaviour. He discovered that newborns had many unique ways of being connected to what was happening around them. He saw that the typical newborn manages stress by shutting down – either turning away or falling asleep. From this observation he realised that how a baby responds to stimulation tells us a lot about her innate temperament. Shutting down was also not seen as negative. In fact, it was seen as very positive; the beginning of self-regulation. Brazelton was convinced that if we could find better ways to tune in to what our infants were doing, we could better understand their experiences and support their development. Studies have also consistently indicated that, *if parents understand their child's temperament, the child will handle big feelings much better.*

Children show us their likes and dislikes, their talents and strengths through their behaviour. We only have to sit back, give them a moment and watch closely for them to reveal themselves to us. Your child behaves in unique ways, whether he is playing, eating, sleeping, going on outings or interacting with you and his peers.

As parents we should act as "detectives". Wait, watch and wonder – your child will soon show you who he truly is. Observe how he moves, how he talks, how he responds when you discipline him and how he responds when he has to face changes and/or stressful situations. Observing our children's behaviour will provide insight into their unique and individual sensory temperament.

# Sensory temperaments

Temperament is what makes all humans unique in how they respond to the world around them. Early research found that infants could be divided into three groups: *easy, difficult* and *slow-to-warm*. The degree to which your child is aware of and reacts to various sensations is an innate part of her temperament. We could call this the child's unique sensory threshold. Returning to the analogy of fuel tanks there are children with

- a small tank that requires only a small amount of fuel to fill up;
- a big tank that requires a considerable amount of fuel to fill up; and
- a large tank that needs frequent filling up as the child is somewhat of a gas guzzler.

This is the foundation on which the theory of sensory temperament has developed. In an attempt to make this theory accessible, understandable and parent-friendly, I'm describing the three sensory temperaments as characterised by three different animals. I find that using these analogies makes it easier for parents and children alike to relate to the concept.

# The three unique sensory temperaments

Your child's appearance and the way in which he acts are as unique as his fingerprints. Some children like to be on the go – moving and touching – always seeking out opportunities to be with others and interact with the world around them. These children are much like **monkeys** – always on the go and actively exploring the world around them. Other children are more laid-back and happy to sit and watch or play with whatever and whomever they can find. **Giraffes,** with their slow movements, remind me of these kids who tend to be slightly under-responsive. Then there are the children who are sensitive and highly attuned to the people and world around them. These children can become easily overloaded in the busy and noisy world that we live in. Just like a **hedgehog**, when they feel threatened they can curl up in a tight ball with all their spines pointing outwards.

## Three unique toddlers

Four-year-old **Sarah** is a sweet little girl. She suffered from colic and her mum, Ruth, remembers how she spent hours walking up and down their corridor in an effort to calm her down. Ruth battled for months to get Sarah into an eating and feeding routine – all she did was short cat-naps during the day and at night she needed a very quiet and dark room to fall asleep. Now that Sarah is a toddler she loves her routine. She has always been a picky eater and fussy about what clothes she wants to wear, although when she finds her favourites she could wear them for days on end. Although it took some time for her to settle into playgroup and nursery school she is a sensitive and caring friend. When the family find themselves in busy or noisy environments, she complains, but she seems happy in calm, quiet places where she shows great focus on a particular task.

She is at her happiest when she can play outdoors and in nature, enjoying her own company.

**Jonathan** was an angelic baby who seldom cried and settled into a feeding and sleeping pattern within the first few weeks and had no trouble falling asleep anywhere – in the pram, in the car or in his cot. When he approached three years his mum felt that she should start potty training him, because he didn't show any inclination of doing it spontaneously. But by the end of that summer they hadn't made much progress and Jonathan needed constant reminders to go to the toilet for several more months. Now almost five, Jonathan does not seem to have a sense of urgency about anything – he needs several reminders to stop playing and get dressed, to eat his food, to get out of the bath and to get into the car. He hardly ever cries or complains – even when he hurts himself – and although he seldom says that he is hungry or thirsty, he eats whatever is offered without complaints. Settling quickly at nursery school, Jonathan seldom talks about friends. When they come to play, he is happy to follow their lead (even with his own toys and in his own room) or play on his own.

**Jack** is a typical five-year-old in many ways. He is inquisitive, extremely alert and always on the go. He was walking confidently before he turned a year and reaches all his milestones early. He has an insatiable need to touch, taste, smell, bang and squish everything he can lay his hands on. Everywhere his family goes, he seems to be the happiest, loudest and busiest child.

Jack wakes up in the morning, alert and ready for an action-packed day, chatting about anything and everything while getting dressed for school, eating breakfast and brushing his teeth – all at the same time. He loves giving their golden retriever big bear hugs and stroking her and demands eight deep hugs from his mum when she greets him at the school gate. He has loads of friends at school and immediately runs off to join them on the monkey bars, shouting that he saw a helicopter on the way to school.

In the late afternoon, Jack joins his mum on her daily run, virtually setting the pace. They hop-skip one block, sprint downhill and climb rocks – all in one run.

**CAN YOU IDENTIFY THE SENSORY TEMPERAMENT OF EACH CHILD?**
Sensitive Sarah fits the characterisation of a hedgehog. Jonathan is under-responsive – a giraffe. And then there is Jack – obviously a monkey – a sensory seeking child.

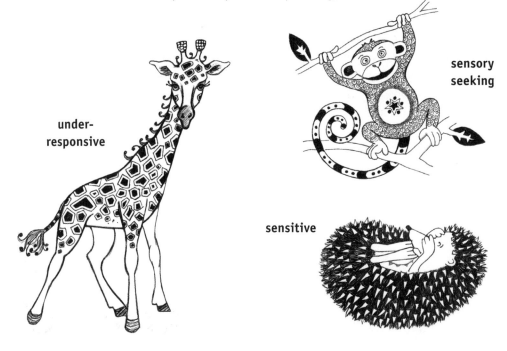

under-
responsive

sensory
seeking

sensitive

**Important facts about sensory temperament:**

**One is not better than another**

No one sensory temperament is better or more ideal than another. Each has its advantages and challenges, strengths and weaknesses.

Parenting a sensitive child (a hedgehog) who clings to you at the gate to the nursery school can be challenging, but her sensitivity and capacity for empathy will make her thoughtful, kind and caring towards others. Having a child who is always on the go and keen to explore (a monkey) is hard work, but his ability to take risks can become his biggest asset as a young entrepreneur. You might have to repeat yourself while your under-responsive child (giraffe) is getting dressed or having supper, but his generally laid-back nature will make him easy to be around.

**It is not all or nothing**

You may recognise your child immediately when reading through the discussion of the different temperaments, or you may feel that he is a little bit of this and a little bit of that.

Your child may react differently to *different sensations*, for instance he could be sensitive to sounds (a hedgehog when it comes to auditory stimuli), but he might crave movement (a monkey when it comes to movement).

Your child may also behave differently in *different situations*, *different environments* and at *different times of the day*. Sensitive children (hedgehogs) will be more outgoing when the interaction is slow and the environment is calm. Hedgehogs usually do better early in the morning compared to later in the day after they've been bombarded with sensory stimuli. Sensory cravers (monkeys) will be calm and focused when they are involved in a purposeful activity with a clear beginning and end. The end of the day is often the optimal response period for children who are under-responsive (giraffes) because they benefit from lots of input and stimulation. Children's behaviour may change over time as they develop, but there will be a dominant temperament – one that is present *most of the time*.

# Identifying your child's unique temperament

Let's take an in-depth look at each of the different sensory temperaments. I encourage you to read with intent to identify your child's temperament, while making allowance for his true nature. Since their inherited traits and the environment in which they grow up vary for most children, few will fit the exact blueprint of a single temperament *all* of the time. I'm nevertheless confident that, having read the information on each of the three different temperaments, you will "see" your child in one.

You may also wish to complete the online assessment at www.lizanneduplessis.com.

**Hedgehogs (the sensory-sensitive child)**

Hedgehogs are amazing, sensitive creatures. Thousands of stiff, sharp spines cover their backs and sides, like a pincushion filled with needles. When hedgehogs feel threatened, they curl up into a tight ball, with their spines sticking out in all directions. When they are out at night, they use regular pathways (preferring sameness and predictability) and are dependent on their highly developed senses of smell and hearing. When the correct techniques are used, a hedgehog will relax and allow handling.

## Know your hedgehog

**Sensory threshold:** *Sensitive*
**Attributes:** *Sensitive, attentive and thoughtful*
**Signs of dysregulation:** *Overly sensitive, overly controlling, anxious, negative, withdrawal*
**Regulation tools:** *Low and slow*

Hedgehog children are sensitive, attentive and thoughtful, preferring predictability and sameness. The wonderful thing about them is that they are finely attuned – they miss nothing. They are able to pick up on the detail in the world around them. They are able, often from a very early age, to "read between the lines" and interpret facial expression and body language. Their capacity for empathy is admirable.

## Hedgehogs

- Seem to be very intuitive.
- Notice others – will be aware if people around them are happy or distressed (might be affected if other babies or children are crying).
- Notice visual detail in their environment – will notice what you are wearing, when you've moved the furniture around.
- Notice differences in textures – whether it is in clothing, food or surfaces on which they walk
- Tend to feel the texture of clothes before putting them on and may ask for labels in clothing to be removed.
- Prefer smooth textures in food (dislike yoghurt with solid pieces of fruit inside).
- Are easily troubled by fluffy, furry, sticky and gooey textures.
- Are aware of sounds in their environment – might hear the aeroplane flying over before you do.

- Tend to startle easily when hearing loud sudden noises such as sirens, hand-dryers or dogs barking.
- Tend to become easily overwhelmed in noisy, busy places.
- Enjoy playing outside.
- Enjoy playing on their own or within a small group of children.
- Think carefully before doing something, demonstrating good impulse control even from a young age.
- Are sensitive to pain and may overreact to minor cuts and bruises.
- May complain initially about the sand at the beach and the noise of the waves, but have the potential to get used to it.
- May dislike and complain about grooming activities such as hair washing, showering and/or hair and nail cutting.
- May dislike or avoid being upside down or going on fast or spinning playground equipment.
- Are upset by change in routines and transitions.
- Do not embrace surprises, especially in unfamiliar environments.

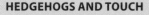

**HEDGEHOGS AND TOUCH**

Your little hedgehog may be oversensitive to touch – especially during times when they are overwhelmed, anxious and/or stressed. Unexpected and light touch will overwhelm a sensitive child. A granny, teacher or friend unexpectedly touching her from behind or touching the top of her head, or light touch such as a kiss or a brush against her arm or body, could be uncomfortable and send a hedgehog's brain into overdrive.

What could be confusing is the fact that these children are often not unaffectionate. They may come and lean into you for hugs and ask for a back rub at bedtime. But these types of touch are not only firm and deep, but also expected – the child asks for it, controls it and is able to prepare her brain and body for what is coming.

When they touch objects and surfaces, in all likelihood these will be soft and smooth – therefore soothing and comforting. They may also like holding on to a special object (such as their comfort blankie or a favourite toy) for extended periods of time, perhaps in an effort to gain some comfort, predictability and control in an ever-changing world with all its unexpected touch experiences.

## Hedgehog babies

A hedgehog baby is simply more sensitive to sounds and will startle easily when she hears a sudden noise like a dog barking, a door slamming or a parent sneezing. When she is touched, she can pull away from you, dislike nappy changes and bathtimes, the feel of the breast, dummy or bottle in her mouth, the texture and touch of clothes and blankets against her body. She dislikes movement, like being turned on her back for a nappy change.

She may need more help to calm down as hedgehogs often don't learn to self-soothe as early and easily as other babies. She may have more trouble settling into routines, but once these have been established she thrives on them.

Transitions and changes in routines are more difficult to deal with and could result in fussiness, irritability and crying.

She may very well suffer from what is commonly known as colic – excessive crying for extended periods of time due to overstimulation.

## Hedgehog toddlers

They are gentle and are usually great friends. Some can be quite bossy and controlling.

They often become dependent on their daily routine and structure, and may develop certain fixed ways of going about things. They may insist on Mummy reading a specific book (always the same one) before going to bed every evening. Transitions are difficult, so stopping play for bathtime may cause meltdowns.

They react to subtle smells in the environment and don't like mess; they will avoid finger painting and playing with sticky mud.

They may have more difficulty separating from Mum when dropped off at nursery school and unfamiliar settings.

They are creatures of habit and changes in routine are often met with a certain amount of resistance.

They may have more difficulty falling asleep.

## Hedgehogs at school

They thrive on predictable routines. When things change, for instance a school trip, sports day or school concert or play, they find it harder to remain calm. Too much unstructured play may be more difficult to manage.

Minor changes, such as new pyjamas, may trigger meltdowns. Big changes, such as starting school, cause anxiety and often some regression in development (thumb-sucking or obsessive attachment to their comfort toy/blankie).

## Hedgehogs as adults

Adults with this temperament are creatures of comfort, routine and structure. The predictability of the routines keeps them contained.

Hedgehog parents are attentive to their children, and to their needs and environment.

When too much is going on, they tend to feel overwhelmed. They tend to become anxious, stressed and fearful when too many demands are made on them and may avoid the situation by withdrawing.

Adult hedgehogs need lots of quiet time to organise themselves, and generally don't cope very well with having too many children in and around the house.

# Parenting a hedgehog

Not all sensitive children behave the same – some are more difficult to parent than others. I've consulted to lots of mums who feel worn out and overwhelmed by the intensity of their hedgehog child's behaviour. They complain that "everything is a crisis" and call their child a "drama queen". Others find it frustrating to deal with the inflexibility of their hedgehog.

## When hedgehogs become overwhelmed

- They respond with aggression or impulsivity, or avoiding the activities altogether.
- They attempt to control everything, from what they wear and what they eat to which games they play.
- They tend to over-respond – the intensity and the duration of their response is too much, too long.

Overload activates the alarm system in a sensitive child's brain, which results in a fight-or-flight response. When having to do finger painting a child who is oversensitive to touch sensations may reach out and carefully put her fingers in the paint. As she touches it, the cold, gooey texture may trigger an exaggerated response in her brain, one or both of the following:

- A **fight response** where she pushes the paint away, hits and/or cries – behaviour that is out of proportion to the task (it's only paint after all – nothing harmful or dangerous and certainly not calling for such a fuss).
- A **flight response** where she refuses to participate or tries vigorously to get the paint off her hands or gets away from the task as soon as possible.

## Other challenges

They tend to overreact to minor stressors (sweating the small stuff). They are prone to worrying and may be short-tempered. Some tend to see the negative side of life – the glass is always half-empty. The heightened alarm system in their brain may make it difficult to manage stress. If they do not learn to self-calm effectively they will be more prone to anxiety, depression and shyness.

## Meeting their needs

Hedgehogs do best when tasks, interactions and environments are safe, calm and predictable. **Low! Slow!** That's the rule of the game when you see that your child is heading towards the red zone (overstimulation leading to dysregulation). Work around sensitivities. If you know that your child doesn't do well when the car radio is on, switch it off. Create a safe place, a den, a quiet corner where she goes when she feels overwhelmed or needs to calm down and recharge.

My younger daughter is a typical hedgehog and life with her as a young toddler was not always easy. Transitions and changes in daily routines notably affected her, resulting in moaning, complaining and meltdowns. By the age of four, she was able to use words to describe her thoughts and feelings, likes and dislikes, which made life much easier. At her school's annual sports day, she spent most of the day crying and said, "This is the worst day ever *because it is so different.*" The change in routine completely threw her. The excitement ten minutes ahead of her fifth birthday party ended up in a meltdown, with her saying: "I don't want to go to my party, because I know it will not be the way that I expect it to be." She benefits enormously from consistent routines and predictability. Mothering a sensitive child can be a challenge, but together we've found great ways to deal with this, like giving her choices as much as possible, preparing for upcoming changes and increasing predictability as far as possible. I once got this written note from her:

*Dear Mum. Tomorrow don't shout at me even if I don't do what you say. If you are going to shout at me, tick this box.*

I'd like to point out that I don't *usually* shout at my children, but what feels like shouting to her is often just me raising my voice a few decibels or adjusting my tone. I love the way that in a sense she gives me permission "to shout", as long as she is prepared for it. This handwritten note shows the importance of predictability to my little hedgehog.

Being intentional about how you parent your sensitive child is hugely important. Research indicates that parenting determines whether being sensitive will be an advantage or a source of anxiety. **Hedgehogs need responsive, sensitive parents who embrace their positive traits and step in when things overwhelm them;** this in turn will reduce the fight-or-flight responses in the brain.

## The giraffe (the under-responsive child)

With their incredibly long legs, big eyes and beautiful patterned coat (which is unique, just like our finger prints), giraffes have only two ways of moving: a looping walk and a gallop. They are quiet animals and don't make much noise although they will grunt or snort when alarmed, and moo when distressed. They are not territorial and move around on their own or in herds from two to fifty. An individual giraffe can join or leave the herd at any time and for no particular reason. Giraffes are probably one of the most chilled out and laid-back creatures on this planet.

## Know your giraffe

*Sensory threshold:* Under-responsive
*Attributes:* Easy-going, flexible
*Signs of dysregulation:* Shut down, unmotivated
*Regulation tools:* Fast and blast

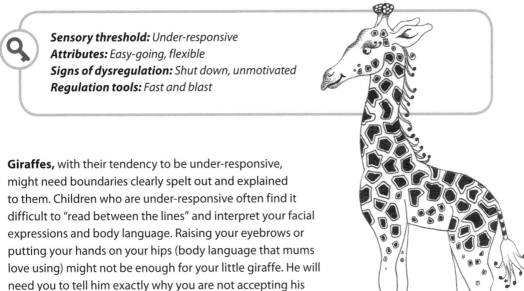

**Giraffes,** with their tendency to be under-responsive, might need boundaries clearly spelt out and explained to them. Children who are under-responsive often find it difficult to "read between the lines" and interpret your facial expressions and body language. Raising your eyebrows or putting your hands on your hips (body language that mums love using) might not be enough for your little giraffe. He will need you to tell him exactly why you are not accepting his behaviour and what you expect of him.

## Giraffes

- Are laid-back and easy-going.
- Rarely complain and are flexible and cope well with changes in routine.
- Are content with their own company and in that of others.
- Prefer solitary and sedentary play.
- Enjoy reading, playing on computers and watching TV.
- Enjoy being outside, but do not initiate running around.
- Can take longer to potty-train because of them being unaware that their bladder is full.
- Don't show discomfort when they have a soiled nappy.
- Are not fussy eaters and will eat hot and spicy food without complaint.
- Are not bothered by minor injuries and appear not to notice bruises and cuts.
- Often don't respond if touched and need commands and instructions to be repeated.
- Are often unaware that it is hot or cold, and need reminders to dress accordingly.
- Don't notice or are not bothered by noxious smells.
- Don't notice if their faces or clothes are wet or dirty.

## Giraffe babies

They are easy babies. They settle into feeding and sleeping routines easily and are generally very content.

They are generally able to nap and sleep in noisy restaurants and nurse wherever you happen to be. They may take a little longer than other babies to achieve their developmental milestones, such as rolling, sitting, crawling and walking.

## Giraffe toddlers

Their parents rarely complain about challenging behaviour or that their toddlers are too busy and active.

## Giraffes at school

They are not usually disruptive in class.

They may take a long time to make friends and when they do they will have only one or two close friends.

## Giraffe adults

They are mostly easy-going and generally more on the quiet side.

They are flexible parents and cope well with the changes that babies and children bring. They don't easily get flustered when the house is full of children and their household that doesn't run on a strict routine – meal times and bedtimes are not set in stone.

They usually take a little longer to leave the house when going out, and may leave things behind – they often battle with organisation and planning.

# Parenting a giraffe

As is the case with hedgehogs, not all giraffes behave the same. Some tend to be lethargic or withdrawn, while others could be dreamy or self-absorbed. This leads to different challenges in all aspects of their development. The biggest challenge in parenting a hedgehog is to avoid situations of overload. With a giraffe, the biggest challenge is to provide enough stimulation.

Withdrawn children may not seek out social interaction and may be quite content to play alone. In extreme cases the biggest challenge is probably their lack of social engagement. They seldom initiate activities and lack the general drive to do things that require physical effort. They will join their friends in play, but will seldom initiate it.

A big concern is that a giraffe may get lost or overlooked in the classroom. They are often described as shy or quiet, when, in fact, their quiet behaviour has nothing to do with shyness but could indicate a lack of focus, which should be discussed with teachers if necessary. They may get bumped, bruised or hurt, but fail to notice it, so their parents need to be on the lookout for evidence of injuries.

A giraffe needs to be hurried up and encouraged to complete tasks.

## Meeting their needs

Giraffes benefit when tasks, interactions and environments are fun, engaging and enticing. Provide an element of unpredictability and stimulate their interest and energy.

**Fast! Blast!** That's the rule of the game when you see that your child's arousal is low. Intense movement or touch activities, such as tickling and rough housing in the morning before getting dressed and chewing on crunchy carrots on the way to school will wake up the giraffe and ensure that he is in the green zone – ready to engage, learn and socialise.

Being intentional about how you parent your under-responsive child can make a huge difference in his levels of focus and activity. Children who have an under-responsive sensory temperament are usually described as lethargic or withdrawn, dreamy or self-absorbed. They rarely move fast, so encourage activities that will engage her muscles: ask her to help carry the groceries from the car, join you for a walk or play jumping games such as hop scotch or take her to the park to swing and climb and run around.

Giraffe children tend to have a smaller but intense range of interests and can get stuck on activities that they really enjoy, like Lego, computers or books. Offer them a wider range to try.

Your dreamy child may create a rich and elaborate fantasy world in which she can get lost. Play along, but encourage real-time games too.

## The monkey (the over-responsive child)

Monkeys typically don't keep still for long periods of time. They are forever exploring on the ground, up and down trees, poking and pulling to investigate everything in their surroundings. They are agile and always on the move – walking, running, hanging, climbing, jumping, swinging and gliding – using their arms, legs and even their tails. At Monkey World (Ape Rescue Centre UK) keepers found that if the monkeys didn't have enough stimulation during the day, they became destructive, challenging and hyperactive. They would break the antennas and wipers off cars and aggressive behaviour between them would increase in frequency and intensity. Monkey World came up with a great solution – a huge climbing frame made out of logs into which they drilled holes strategically placed all over the climbing construction. The monkeys' food was placed in these holes, which meant that they spent an extended period of time finding their food, instead of having it readily accessible in a container. In this process, they were climbing up and down and swinging back and forth. As a result their behaviour improved – they were calmer and less destructive and aggressive.

## Know your monkey

*Sensory threshold:* Seeking
*Attributes:* Active, inquisitive, social
*Signs of dysregulation:* Overactive ("hyper"), distractable
*Regulation tools:* Goal-orientated, purposeful, stop and start

In general, young children are active and love to run and jump, much more than we as adults do. We encourage active exploration and know that this is the foundation for learning and development. But compared to children with other sensory temperaments, monkeys need much more – **more movement, more touch, more sounds, more intense tastes,** or whatever it might be. **Monkeys seek intense sensations that last for a long time.**

## Monkeys

- Are excitable and energetic.
- Enjoy jumping, crashing, banging, and spinning.
- Enjoy being with lots of friends.
- Find creative ways to play.
- Frequently come up with new ideas.
- Enjoy novelty and change and positively accept transitions.
- Are talkative.
- Are curious and open to new experiences.
- Are affectionate and like big bear hugs.
- Are daring and risk takers.
- Have a high level of perseverance.

## Monkey babies

You will describe your monkey baby as mostly alert and happy – smiling and interacting with everyone – from family members to strangers at the park.

Monkeys do well when they are swaddled really tightly, since they crave the deep-pressure touch that swaddling provides.

They are generally quick to reach their physical milestones, especially when it comes to crawling, walking and climbing.

They enjoy being tossed into the air.

## Monkey toddlers

They find change interesting. They enjoy new interactions, like a new baby-sitter and new environments.

They like new clothes or toys, and would not complain even if you move the furniture in their bedroom around.

They tend to be daring, and will climb, swing, run and jump in ways that could be dangerous to them. When playing they make lots of noise, shriek often and prefer interactive toys that make sounds.

They may find sharing and taking turns challenging, because they don't like waiting.

Calming down for an afternoon nap or at bedtime may be challenging.

## Monkeys at school

They are often the class clowns and find it hard to stay in their seats. They fidget excessively when asked to sit still.

Their constant need for movement and touch may be disruptive in the classroom environment. When their sensory needs aren't met, they can become aggressive and explosive.

They often enjoy eating spicy and acidic food, such as curries, salsa or Tabasco sauce.

They enjoy listening to loud music.

They may have trouble organising themselves and tasks, so morning routines including multistep tasks, such as getting dressed, are difficult.

They lack personal space awareness and will sit and stand and play close to other children, readily touching them.

## Monkey adults

Adults who fit this temperament are the ones who seldom sit still. They are always on the go and never do just one thing at a time.

They have lots of energy, like being busy and out and about, and therefore easily become frustrated with set routines and rituals.

They can also be described as adrenaline junkies who aren't afraid of trying new things (often without carefully considering the consequences).

As mums, they embrace having a busy home environment and having more than one child.

They are huggers and often touch others while interacting with them.

**MONKEYS AND TOUCH**

Monkeys seek more touch than children who are hedgehogs or giraffes – more deep pressure, more skin contact and more fiddling. They go around touching everything they see – walls, furniture, toys, fragile ornaments and people. No matter how hard they try to control themselves, they simply *have to* touch and will sometimes put non-food objects into their mouths past the normal developmental age. They learn about things in their environment by feeling them. Using only their eyes to figure out how heavy, light, smooth or rough something is, is simply not enough. Even as adults, monkeys just have to touch.

**MONKEYS AND MOVEMENT**

Your monkey's brain needs more intense and more frequent movement, therefore he tends to crave movements that do exactly that – he climbs higher and jumps for longer than you would expect. Slow, rhythmical forwards and backwards swinging is not enough – your monkey will find ways to increase the pace – he will rock, pull and push on the ropes of the swing or even try to hang upside down while shouting out: "More! More! Higher! Higher!"

## Parenting a monkey

When monkeys' sensory needs aren't met, they behave in challenging ways that are often difficult for parents, caregivers and teachers to manage. Sometimes their intense craving for sensory input interferes with their ability to stay calm and focused. Your child might be so driven to feed his hunger for movement or touch that he will not be able to get dressed, brush his teeth or finish his plate of food. These children, when dysregulated, are often the ones that are labelled naughty, destructive and hyperactive. Their affection, curiosity and creativity are admirable, but at times their inability to stop, their constant fidgeting and daring, make it difficult to be around them.

Outings can be challenging as monkeys tend to be impulsive and easily distracted by everything going on around them. They may find it difficult to focus on one thing at a time – bouncing from the swing to the slide to the monkey bars in an effort to experience the sensation that each provides, and jump the queue without realising it. At times your monkey is able to come up with creative ideas to make ordinary, daily routines less boring, but at other times his behaviour is over the top because of his craving for sensations (especially movement and touch).

Standing in queues, waiting for appointments, sitting still in a place of worship, family gatherings in small spaces and rainy days – these are the times when your monkey will be most challenging and the times when he is likely to need extra support. Without this, he may become dysregulated.

## Meeting their needs

The most important parenting strategy for children who are sensory seekers is to create opportunities for movement while ensuring they require enough heavy work and have a goal, a purpose and a clear beginning and end. Telling a sensory seeker to run outside just to let off steam will not do the trick. Whenever possible, add a goal to an activity: "When the sand has run through the timer, I want you to have your shirt, short and shoes on." "Jump twenty times on the trampoline and then come and tag me." "Let's swing thirty times and then we'll go home."

Being intentional about how you parent your over-responsive child can help him channel his abundance of energy into well-chosen activities to calm down and remain focused. He benefits when tasks, interactions and environments are:
◀ goal orientated
◀ provide an element of fun and novelty
◀ provide opportunities for touching and moving.

Jack's mum knows the power of letting him do wheelbarrow-walking to the bathroom for brushing teeth, giving him a big exercise ball to sit on instead of a chair and placing his clothes on the highest shelf so that he has to climb onto a stepladder to get them. Life for them is never dull and her creativity is tested, but it is lots of fun!

Calming aromatherapy oils in a burner, lots of hugging, stories with bright and colourful illustrations and a textured cuddly toy at bedtime will also work wonders to help your monkey wind down before going to sleep.

Children are nowadays labelled at the drop of a hat. Do take care that your bouncy monkey is not too readily diagnosed as suffering from ADHD and treated with medication when all he needs is for his needs to be considered, and fulfilled with structured stimulation.

Read more about ADHD on my website www.lizanneduplessis.com.

Jack's mum *gets* it. She appreciates that life with a monkey is busy and active and fun, and that she may have a dysregulated monkey on her hands unless she helps meet his sensory needs.

But it wasn't always smooth sailing for her or for Jack. "Having a monkey as my first-born was a massive learning curve!" she says. "Parenting a child like Jack in Europe with its indoor lifestyle was not easy. I left many play dates and children's parties feeling alone, helpless and like I'm the worst parent ever. I was confronted with questions such as, 'Why can he not sit still when other children of his age seem to manage it?' 'Why is he always the one that seems to be behaving like a bull in a china shop?' It was only after I heard about sensory processing and the unique sensory temperaments that I realised how hard Jack has to work to keep it all together. He was expected to sit still on the carpet or in church or in a waiting room – and he just couldn't! His whole body was desperately shouting, 'I need to move!' But he didn't have the words or the self-awareness to tell the world. It wasn't that he didn't try to do the things expected of him. At times I saw in his little face how desperately he wanted to please me or the teacher or whoever, but his need for sensory input was overwhelming."

# Be your child's champion

Remember that one temperament is not better than another. The goal is not to change your monkey, giraffe or hedgehog into something else. The goal is to develop an awareness of your child's unique sensory temperament and help him to make the most of it, by embracing his strengths and supporting his weaknesses.

You can also help others – siblings, teachers and grandparents – to understand your child better. When your hedgehog is avoiding eye contact with her new teacher and resists any physical touch, you can explain, "Sophie, like a lot of other children, is a bit like a hedgehog. She needs less touching and talking and just some extra time. When she is ready she will show you her beautiful face." Then go down to Sophie's level and show the teacher how you just sit quietly next to her, and how to approach her slowly and gently.

You can also help your children to understand their friends better. This will strengthen their relationships and teach them great skills, such as empathy, mutual respect and unconditional acceptance. A hedgehog might find a monkey sitting next to her on the carpet very difficult to deal with, as the encroachment on her personal space and the intensity of the monkey's movements will lead to unexpected touch input.

Once children understand the different temperaments, it is remarkable to see how they are able to accommodate each other. They move away from monkeys, approach hedgehogs softly and grab the giraffe by the hand to get him to join their play.

Developing a tolerance for the challenges that face each temperament is important within families. Read my conversation with my older daughter (who is mostly a giraffe and a little bit of a hedgehog) at their school's annual sports day. This was the day throughout which my younger daughter, my little hedgehog, cried.

"Why is Cara crying so much?"

"This is her first sports day. She doesn't really know what she should be doing and how it all works."

"But I didn't cry all day long when it was my first."

"You were brave, I remember that. But remember Cara is a little hedgehog. Little hedgehogs like it when things are the same. When things aren't the same, they can get upset."

Lize was quiet for a moment.

"Okay," she said, "I hope that next year she'll like it, because then she'll know what to do. It's fun!"

And so it came, another sports day, a year later. On the way to school I could hear Cara whispering to herself, "I can do this, I can do this, I can do this." She managed really well and got through the sports day without any tears, or having to cling onto me. I wouldn't say she loved it, but we were all very proud of how well she did.

The analogy of animals seems to work really well to make children understand their friends. On our way to a birthday party at an indoor playground we talked about which of my girls' friends would be there (a good way of preparing sensitive hedgehogs for the chaos and intense input of these events).

After naming a few children, I asked them which animals they thought each of the children was. I was blown away and amazed by their ability to identify the monkeys, giraffes and hedgehogs among their friends.

What I found very encouraging was the fact that they were able to do this without passing any judgement on any of the different temperaments. It was a reminder that, if we understand why people do things the way they do, it will enrich our relationships.

# Is there more to my child's behaviour than meets the eye?

Let's face it – all of us have certain likes and dislikes, weird and wonderful ways of doing things, and they are what make all of us unique. But when should you be asking yourself,

"Is my child's behaviour simply part of her sensory temperament, or is it becoming a problem?"

There may be times when your child asks you to cut all the labels out of her clothes, or might not be able to sit still in your place of worship or wait patiently in the queue at the bank. These behaviours do not affect every aspect of her daily life or get in the way of her development.

However, if your child's behaviour – whether he is a monkey, hedgehog or giraffe – is chronic and disrupts his everyday life, you should consider the possibility that he has Sensory Processing Disorder (SPD). These children often get "stuck" and, no matter how creative and determined you are as a parent – no matter how many star charts, stickers, bribes or punishment you use – a child with SPD finds it really hard to ignore the responses triggered by his oversensitivity, under-sensitivity or sensory craving. Children with SPD expend a great deal of energy every day compensating for out-of-sync sensory systems.

For more information on SPD, please go to my website www.lizanneduplessis.com.

# PART II

..........................................

# Ingredients that grow happy children

# The glue that keeps it all together

........................................................................

*"Did you ever stop to think, and forget to start again?" – Pooh*

– A.A. Milne, *Winnie-the-Pooh*

Toddlerhood is an exciting time – a time of great growth and development. So much is happening in those little bodies and brains. Self-regulation is the ability to manage what we feel, think and do. It is the glue that helps us to keep it all together. **Self-regulation is the foundation for everything we do.** It affects our relationships and interaction with the world. It is what makes us feel calm, connected and happy.

Self-regulation is a skill that develops over time and something at which we have to work hard for the rest of our lives. It's not only hard for us as adults. It is exceptionally hard for toddlers whose brains are still in the process of maturing. As we've seen in Chapter 2, the toddler's brain, and especially the part that operates the brakes, controls the impulses and regulates the body and emotions, is far from developed. No wonder the "terrible two's" and "toddler tantrums" are some of the most discussed topics. It all comes down to that complex and highly sophisticated skill called self-regulation.

In this chapter we will take a brief look at some aspects of self-regulation. We'll discuss what effective self-regulation looks like, which strategies we use to regulate and how we can help our children develop this vital skill.

I remember a bitterly cold and windy day in Delft, The Netherlands. It was past my little girl's nap time when I finally managed to get to the local grocery store. She moaned when I put her in the car seat, and even more when I took her out and strapped her into the stroller, but it was a full-blown angry cry when I finally managed to get her seated in the shopping trolley. Hats, scarves, mittens and boots were flying everywhere. I need some glue, I thought. I'll glue those mittens on because I need them to stay on those little hands. Just for now. It's cold and I need to do the shopping. At the end of what was the most disastrous shopping experience ever, I remember thinking that I needed more than just plain glue. I needed superglue. We were both in pieces. She was so tired and there was nothing I could do to calm her. It was another one of those unglued moments.

The ability to self-regulate is considered an essential part of children's healthy emotional development and is increasingly regarded as a good predictor of a child's academic success.

In Chapter 1 we spoke about the brain being like a specialised thermostat, striving to maintain *a comfort zone* – that *just-right place* where we feel calm, happy and able to connect with the world and people around us. Sportsmen, artists, writers – anybody who is using a special skill and aiming for a specific goal – often talk about *being in the zone*. And they have a positive association with *the zone*. It feels good to be there, they can get things done and they feel happy. But we don't just automatically get in the zone. Our bodies and brains have to work constantly to get us there and keep us there.

## The green zone

This is the optimal zone in which we would like to spend most of our waking hours. In this zone we get things done and operate effectively. When our children are in this zone, they can learn, progress and make sense of what is going on around them. When in this zone your child looks and feels:

- Calm
- Connected
- Happy
- Focused
- Mindful
- Attentive
- Content

## The danger zone

When your child is in this zone he starts to moan, may become cranky and irritable. He yawns, may start to hiccup and/or disengage. Your child looks and feels:

- Frustrated
- Upset
- Whiny
- Clingy
- Nervous
- Stressed
- Silly/Clowning
- Fidgety
- Bored/Distractible
- Reluctant
- Saying, "No, I won't!"
- Increasingly impulsive
- Over-sensitive

When your child is in this zone he needs to find ways to regulate and restore balance. At times he might be able to do it independently (especially an older toddler who will take himself off to a quiet corner to read or play quietly). Other times he might need your help in finding ways to restoring balance. When these prove successful, your child will move back to the green zone. There will, however, be times when, for whatever reason, the strategies don't work. Then your child will move into the red zone.

## The red zone

For some children this means shutting down and isolating themselves. For others dysregulation leads to impulsive, overactive, aggressive or oversensitive behaviour. You child looks and feels:

- Explosive
- Erratic
- Aggressive
- Sleepy
- Angry
- Impulsive
- Withdrawn
- Crying inconsolably

When your child is in this zone, his survival brain takes over and he reverts to primitive behaviour. He might kick, scream, bite or do things that are completely out of character. When your child's brain is in such a state of fight or flight, you need to actively help him to restore balance. This is not the time to talk, lecture or teach.

# Self-regulation is an acquired skill

Teaching children ways to regulate their bodies, thoughts and feelings is a great art. Some days you'll feel that you've nailed it, but then there are others when you just can't get your child (or yourself) out of that danger zone. The following are important reminders:

## Self-regulation develops over time

Children aren't born with the ability to self-regulate – it develops over time.

As your child grows from infancy to adulthood, so his regulation skills develop and mature. That means that our parenting plays a huge part in helping our children develop, practise and finally achieve the goal of *self*-regulation.

In the first year your baby moves from being fully reliable on you and other caregivers to soothe her and establish feeding and sleeping cycles, to being able to self-soothe and fall asleep without your help.

As adults we help our babies and young toddlers by being their *co-regulator*. We soothe them by picking them up, rocking them, holding them tight and using a calming voice. We use distraction when dealing with distressing situations, such as vaccinations or bouts of separation anxiety.

As he grows older, your toddler will develop the ability to *self*-regulate. He will find it easier to stay focused on a task and calm himself when he gets upset or dysregulated. There will be lots of times when he still needs your help, especially when dealing with intense feelings such as frustration, sadness, joy and excitement.

## Some need more help than others

Some children need more help (coaching and practising) when it comes to learning and developing effective self-regulation skills. Some children just can't seem to stay long enough in the green zone. They find it difficult to stay calm and connected and are affected by changes in the environment (distractions) or by their own sensory needs (their craving or avoidance of sensory input).

## Effective self-regulation

Self-regulation is most successful when we use our bodies as well as our thinking. Using our bodies means engaging our senses (including touch, movement, pressure as well as the senses of seeing, hearing, smelling and tasting) to regulate. We breathe deeply, we stretch our bodies, we drink a cup of tea, we go for a run or chew gum – effective strategies to restore the balance in our bodies, feelings and thoughts.

***Super Star Strategies*** are great tools for regulating.

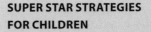

**SUPER STAR STRATEGIES FOR CHILDREN**

- Breathe deeply in and out a few times.
- Stretch your arms and your legs out as far up and wide out as you can.
- Bend down and touch your toes.
- Give yourself a tight hug.

## Thinking

When we talk ourselves through tasks, set goals and remind ourselves why we are doing what we are doing, we activate the thinking part of our brains. These strategies are effective for older children and adults who can focus and concentrate for an extended period of time. As children develop and their thinking brain matures they use increasingly more thinking strategies. Older toddlers are able to use reminders and will talk themselves through tasks. "If I get dressed quickly, I will have more time to play," or "If I finish my dinner, I will get pudding." But this is the area where they still need your help. Until his thinking brain is well developed, a child will not always be able to use his thinking skills successfully and may revert to more primitive patterns. A tired toddler who is dragged to the shops late afternoon is not able to talk himself through the task by thinking: "We are just picking up a few groceries. We'll be home soon." In his attempt to regulate, he uses mainly sensory strategies (because this is all that his immature brain is letting him do). He stretches, he swings his legs, he hangs over the side of the trolley, he tries to touch everything – all in an attempt to regulate.

We only have to look at a company like Google, whose offices are filled with Ping-Pong tables, to know that they have figured out the secret. Our brains need a combination of moving, feeling and thinking to function optimally.

**What happens if my child doesn't develop self-regulation?**
Many kids have difficulty with self-regulation, which could result from many factors including genetic predisposition, difficulties with sensory processing, poor attachment, parental neglect and trauma. Children who battle with self-regulation face many emotional, social and academic challenges including sleep problems, fussy eating, poor mood regulation and self-soothing, aggression, impulsiveness, hypersensitivity to transitions and learning problems.

# Promoting self-regulation

Self-regulation develops with time and practice under the guidance of a parent who is patient, warm and attentive. Think about the time when your parents taught you how to tie your shoelaces. I remember sitting down with my mum and having to do it again and again. Of course, it would have been easier for our parents just to do it for us – it would have saved time – but they didn't. They taught us this skill because they knew that they couldn't do our shoelaces for us for the rest of our lives. We cannot be with our children all day every day for the rest of their lives to help them regulate. But teaching them how to be successful at regulating begins first and foremost with us – the parent, the adult, the teacher, the caregiver. To promote the development of self-regulating skills in your child, you have to:

- be a good role model;
- lower your expectations; and
- show and teach empathy.

## Be a good role model

Children learn by watching us. It is a proven fact that the example we set our children often carries more value than the lessons we are trying to teach them by talking them through tasks, punishments and rewards. We shouldn't be surprised that our children end up doing things exactly the way we do them or saying words or phrases exactly the way we say them. One of my most embarrassing moments as a mum was when the nursery teacher did a home visit and my then two-and-a-half year old said a swear word (the one I don't often say but admittedly have said a few times)! It was like seeing and hearing a mini me – she said it using the exact tone of voice and the same facial expression I do. (Sure enough that was a quick lesson in the need for self-control!)

It is hugely important for our kids to see how hard we are working at regulating our actions, feelings and thoughts. If you use statements such as, "I feel really angry now because that man took my parking space" or ,"I feel frustrated because I can't get this thing to work", and show the anger and frustration in your body language and facial expression, your child will learn so much. He will learn about different emotions and what they look like. He will see that it is okay to express these emotions even if they are "negative". But most importantly they will see and learn some appropriate ways to manage these big feelings.

But staying calm is easier said than done! When we lose self-control, just like toddlers, our primitive brain takes over and we behave just like a two-year-old. Out come the words and actions you vowed you would never say or do (before you had children!). When we are out of control and dysregulated our primitive brain takes over and if we cannot engage the brakes, we:

- Blame: "You are making it so difficult for me!"
- Say hurtful things: "You drive me nuts!" (we use shame in an attempt to change behaviour)
- Focus on the things that we don't want to happen: "You are always making a mess!"
- Get trapped in negative emotions "Why is she always so difficult?", "Why are my children always the ones that cause the chaos at the party?", "Why can't I get my children to go to bed without a drama?"
- Punish without using the opportunity to teach. We send them to their room, we put them on the naughty step, we take the toys away.
- Lose the connection with our children.

The fact is that, even as grown-ups, we don't always manage to keep ourselves well regulated and in control. I have yet to meet the parent who can say in all honesty that they have never lost it. It is okay for your child to see that you, the grown-up, may at times lose it completely (obviously as long as it doesn't happen too often). I challenge you, however, when you do lose it, use the opportunity and restore the relationship. In Brené Brown's words: "… the best teaching moments happen in those imperfect moments when we allow children to help us mind the gap." We say we are sorry and promise to keep trying. "Mummy lost it today. I'm really sorry. I shouldn't have behaved like that. I'll keep on trying to stay calm."

> "The repair we do after the times when things fall
> apart is just as important as the example we set
> when we demonstrate keeping it all together."

## Lower your expectations

Always bear in mind that children develop the full capacity for self-regulation much later than we expect them to do so. As adults we mostly use top-down strategies to regulate and calm ourselves. When we feel disorganised and overwhelmed, we stand up, take a break and breathe deeply, we remind ourselves of our goals (why we are doing what we are doing), we problem-solve and then motivate ourselves to go back and try again – we persevere until we've reached our goal. There is no way that we can expect a two- to three-year-old to do this.

As Selma Fraiberg puts it: *"… we must remember that months and years go into this education [teaching children to use words and thoughts in dealing with impulses] and although we can expect improved control by the end of the third year, [a toddler] is still a pleasure-loving little fellow and lapses in control will be frequent."*

## Show and teach empathy

If it is this challenging for us as parents to keep it all together – to move smoothly through the ups and downs – imagine how difficult it must be for a young developing child who has not yet mastered the capacity to regulate his body, feelings, thinking and responses. We have to try putting ourselves in their shoes. How would *you* feel if your friend breaks your favourite toy and your brain is not helping to reassure you that it's okay? How would *you* feel if you had spent hours constructing a complicated bridge and suddenly it all collapses on you? Surely we would also feel angry and frustrated. Focus on the *feeling* and remind yourself that, if you were in your child's shoes, you might be feeling exactly what he is feeling now. Show empathy for your child by saying things like, "Mummy can see that you are really upset now", "I can understand why you might feel frustrated now" or "It must be really hard".

Children's ability to regulate independently is also greatly affected by their ability to imagine what emotions someone else is experiencing. If your child is able to imagine what it feels like to have his favourite toy snatched from him, he might think twice before he grabs his friend's toy. Ways of teaching our children empathy is by asking them questions like "How do you think it makes Mummy feel if you shout at me like that?"

> **On my journey through and research in the field of self-regulation I have learnt that:**
> - Self-regulation is a "whole-brain skill". It involves capacities such as processing of sensations, ability to control big emotions like fear, anger and frustration, as well as higher cognitive functions such as attention, focus and problem-solving.
> - Self-regulation starts developing early in life and continues to do so right into adulthood – as adults we continue to work on the regulation of our thoughts and feelings, self-control and focus.
> - Self-regulation is an acquired skill. It is an important skill that can be nurtured, developed and enhanced by ordinary parents and teachers through everyday tasks and in normal situations.
> - Play is an important part of developing and improving self-regulation. Make sure that your child has enough time to play, both with and without you.

# 5

# Start moving

........................................................

*"A bear, however hard he tries, grows tubby without exercise."*

– A. A. Milne, *Winnie-the-Pooh*

Children learn and develop through movement. They develop the foundation skills needed for academic functioning, such as reading, writing and maths. They learn how to hold their bodies up against gravity and coordinate big and small movements, and they learn about spatial relationships. But movement is not important only for the development of these skills; it also plays a vital role in the process of regulation and in us feeling happy. In order for your child to regulate his body efficiently, he needs to recognise what it feels like to be calm, revved up and sluggish. He needs to know what is going on inside his body. Only then will he be able to find acceptable ways of regulating it up or down, so that it is appropriate to the situation and time of day.

   In this chapter we look at practical activities to use when teaching our children how to control their bodies and use movement to self-regulate.

# Movement and regulation

Movement is what makes us tick and keeps us ticking. It is one of the magic ingredients that creates balance in the body and prepares the brain for learning. When you need to push your "reset button" and get things "back on track" you need movement. Think about the times when you get back from a long day at work: you are physically and mentally tired, your brain and body feel overworked and overloaded. You drag yourself off to the gym or go for a run, wondering why you are doing it, but when you come back home you know why. You feel better – your brain feels refreshed and your body feels relaxed. The **right type of movement** at the **right time** is crucial for our wellbeing.

Children need more movement than adults. They need movement to be more intense and more frequent, and for it to last longer. Their developing brains need their developing bodies to run, jump and swing more, higher and longer than ours do. Depending on the intensity and duration of movement, its effect on our brains and bodies can last from two to six hours. An hour-long intensive workout at lunch time will keep you going until you go to bed at night. But as a rule of thumb, children should be involved in some movement at least every hour. If you know that your child will be expected to sit still for any length of time, like going on a long car journey, going to the cinema or theatre, standing in a queue or sitting in a waiting room, it is a good idea to do some movement stimulation beforehand. Five to ten minutes of jumping, crawling, rolling and even stretching will regulate him and hopefully last for the duration of the inactive period.

> 🔍 *Movement creates balance. It restores calm and develops our ability to connect and pay attention.*

# What movement does

*Movement can be calming, stimulating or organising (regulating).*

The type of movement and how you do it determine its effect. Fast, irregular movement (such as a rollercoaster ride) is generally stimulating and will wake you up. Slow, rhythmical rocking (for instance lying in a hammock) is generally calming. Movements that activate the **proprioceptive system** (the body position sense) are great regulators and organisers. Think of activities that apply pressure to the joints and muscles – anything that involves pushing, pulling, hanging and holding.

**stimulating**

## Whole-body movements

- Pushing, pulling, holding or carrying heavy objects, such as a box filled with books or toys.
- Basic household chores, such as making the beds, sweeping, raking leaves, digging, hoovering, moving furniture and cleaning windows or the car.
- Outside play on equipment:
  - ◀ Hanging on a trapeze bar
  - ◀ Playing on monkey bars
  - ◀ Pumping a swing
  - ◀ Jumping on a trampoline.

- Obstacle courses do not need to be restricted to the outdoors. On rainy days or in the evening, let go of your urge to keep your house tidy (reminder to self!) and allow your child to use sofas, pillows, chairs, tables, balls and anything he can find to come up with creative and innovative obstacle courses in the house.
  - Wheelbarrow walking is an amazing activity that can be used from an early age. When doing wheelbarrows, your child engages her core, shoulder girdle and hand muscles, which will help her remain calm and focused, and enhances her gross- and fine-motor development. Be creative about when and how to use this activity: do wheelbarrow races inside the house during rainy weather, or do wheelbarrow walking as part of the morning and evening routine.
  - Push-ups and bridges (lying on the back and lifting the pelvis and bottom).
  - Animal walks: leopard crawling, crab walking, bear walking, slithering like a snake.
  - Exercise ball activities are great to do indoors and as a quick "movement snack" for the body.
  - Ride a bicycle, roller skate, roller blade, skateboard or J-board.
  - Rough and tumble.

## On-the-go movement activities

Regulation through movement isn't limited to the big muscle groups. Also include the mouth (the jaw is involved when chewing, sucking and swallowing), the hands and the legs. Examples of these types of movements that will organise your toddler are:
- Pressing, rolling and squeezing play dough, therapy putty or Prestik
- Sucking water from an exercise bottle
- Chewing substances such as gum and dried fruit
- Eating crunchy food, such as apples, raw carrots, pretzels and rice cakes
- Handling brain toys (hand fidgets)

> We all naturally fidget with things in our hands to help us focus. However, the term fidget often has a negative connotation and therefore I prefer to use the term "brain toys" – objects that enhance the ability of the body and the brain to stay calm and attentive. These include stress balls, rubber bands, slinkies, clothes pegs, paper clips and porcupine balls.

## Movement and sensory temperament

When your child's body and brain are out of sync, the movements that you introduce should also fit his unique sensory temperament.

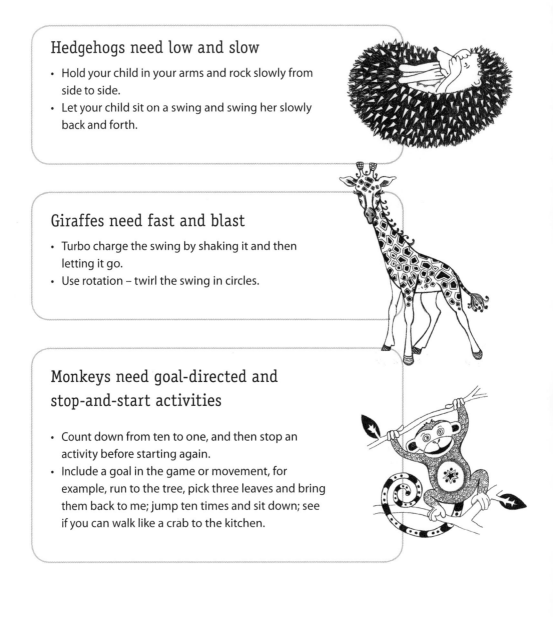

### Hedgehogs need low and slow

- Hold your child in your arms and rock slowly from side to side.
- Let your child sit on a swing and swing her slowly back and forth.

### Giraffes need fast and blast

- Turbo charge the swing by shaking it and then letting it go.
- Use rotation – twirl the swing in circles.

### Monkeys need goal-directed and stop-and-start activities

- Count down from ten to one, and then stop an activity before starting again.
- Include a goal in the game or movement, for example, run to the tree, pick three leaves and bring them back to me; jump ten times and sit down; see if you can walk like a crab to the kitchen.

# Three steps to teach your child to self-regulate

## ( 1 ) Help your child become aware of how his body is feeling

If we can get our children to become aware of what it feels like when their bodies are out of balance – either too revved up or too sluggish – we can help them regulate. Young toddlers will benefit from hearing you say, "My, you are breathing fast. Your heart is beating quickly."

Describe how your body is feeling. Be expressive with your body, your face and your words. Do this a few times throughout the day. "I'm struggling to get out of bed. My body is really floppy", "My tummy is rumbling. I think it needs some food." "I am so excited that we are going to the movies. I feel like my heart wants to pop out of my body." "That slide was fast. It makes my heart beat fast and my body feels happy." "I cannot move this heavy box on my own. I feel really frustrated. I feel like my body wants to explode." "I feel like I have butterflies dancing in my tummy. It's such a strange feeling. I think I'm a little bit worried about being late for the party." Always try to link your feelings to physical experiences in your body – this is very important for your toddler. When appropriate, also come up with possible solutions, such as getting food to calm a hungry tummy.

## ( 2 ) Link your child's behaviour to what you see his body doing

As children develop, they become aware what it feels like for their bodies to be *just right, too high* or *too low*; or *organised, hyper* or *sluggish*. Use creative ways to describe how it feels when your body gets out of balance, and is moving "too fast", "just right" or "too slow". A well-known resource in the field of self-regulation is **The Alert Program** developed by occupational therapists Mary Williams and Sherry Shellenberger. They use the analogy of the body being like an engine to explain how it acts in the regulation process: *"If your body is like a car engine, sometimes it runs on high, sometimes it runs on low, and sometimes it runs just right."* It is helpful to use analogies with children when teaching them self-regulation strategies. The car engine analogy will work for some children, while others may respond better when you talk about *turning the volume up* or *turning it down, making their body go fast like a cheetah* or *slow like a snail*. Every child has a unique way of regulating. If we tap into this, she will feel understood and loved. And even more important, you will empower her to develop self-regulation skills that will stand her in good stead for the rest of her life.

**3** ) Help your child find appropriate ways to regulate his body

The following games work when done regularly and playfully:
- Play "Simon-says" games, with you and your toddler taking turns to be Simon.
- Pillow fights are great as they allow opportunities to experiment with expressing frustration.
- Games that focus on modulating an activity level, e.g. jumping as fast as you can, then medium fast, then slow. Playing games in slow-motion or playing the traffic-light game (as described below) will allow kids to develop a sense of how it feels to move slowly and fast, and how to stop and start – all important components in the ability to self-regulate.

### TRAFFIC-LIGHT GAME

You can play this game as soon as your child can identify colours consistently.

Make a traffic light with red, yellow and green lights.
- Red means *stop* – "stop dead in your track and don't move a muscle"
- Yellow means *think* – "slow down to almost stopping and wait"
- Green means *go* – "carry on marching or running"

Your child marches on the spot or run around the room or garden. You call out the colours and he responds with the appropriate behaviour.

A study by Roger Weissberg assessed social emotional learning programmes, which included games like these, and which involved 270 000 children. His findings indicated better attention and attendance, more liking of school, less misbehaving or substance abuse, and fewer fights. More interesting, perhaps, was that these children's academic achievement scores increased by eleven per cent.

# Case in point: Push-ups for ballet?

Push-ups are not something I'd normally do with kids, but when Dad is at the helm, interesting things happen! It was a rainy Saturday morning in London and time for our little girl's first ballet class. With my little hedgehog anything that has a "first" attached to it could be a challenge. There is usually some dysregulation that plays itself out in anything from tears to anger, reluctance and full-blown meltdown. Today was no exception. When asked to get her leotard on, my husband saw the warning signs that she was heading towards a meltdown.

Suddenly I heard him commanding her in a stern but playful voice, "Ten push-ups please." She immediately stopped complaining and looked at him with a confused expression on her face. But he had her attention – instead of collapsing on the floor in floods of tears because he wanted her to get dressed, she was focusing on him and ready to engage. Now the ball was in his court – if he played this point well, they might just walk off to ballet with a smile; play it wrong and he might have to drag an unhappy little girl there. True to her hedgehog nature, she clearly felt uncertain, worried and overwhelmed at the prospect of this new ballet class. She needed him to help her "reset" and restore calm and happiness. My husband, the genius that he is, chose movement to help him with his mission.

He continued, "Oh, it seems like you don't know what push-ups are? Hmm … that means I will have to catch you … and … tickle you!" He playfully caught her and engaged in some rough-and-tumble play, having her squeal with laughter. After a minute or two of rough and tumble, he stopped and asked if she wanted him to show her how to do a push-up. She happily agreed – most children love to get their dad physically involved, on the floor and moving about. She quickly grasped the concept and managed her ten push-ups well. She carried on doing more and exclaimed, "Look, Daddy, I'm strong, I can do more!" "Oh, but you are strong! I wonder if you would be able to dress yourself too? Is that something that strong girls like you can do as well?"

By now all balance was restored – Cara was calm and engaged and got dressed in a flash. My husband won this round – something that is very good for his self-esteem too! The end results: a four-year-old and a dad both ready to take on the next challenge – the ballet class.

All of this took only about five minutes – remarkable if you consider all the learning that occurred in such a short space of time. If my husband had been feeling under pressure, stressed, or tired after a long week, however, he might have chosen a different approach. He might have said, "I've told you to get dressed. Put on your clothes *now*, or you'll go into time-out." This way he would have completely dismissed her feelings of anxiety and uncertainty. It would have left her feeling unheard, alone and isolated, overwhelmed with big feelings and not yet equipped with the skills to manage and control them. Cara would in all likelihood have done as she was told, but only because she was scared of the consequences. Such behaviour management results in a child feeling misunderstood and possibly also out of control, as well as a frustrated and deflated dad whose only desire was to spend quality time with his daughter. Parenting like this does not contribute in any way to the development of effective self-regulation skills.

# 6

# Start feeling

· · · · · · · · · · · · · · · · · · · · · · · · · · · · · · · · · · · · · · · · · · ·

*"A little consideration, a little thought for others, makes all the difference."*
– A.A. Milne, *Winnie-the-Pooh*

Life brings with it a range of emotions: joy, sadness, anger, love, frustration, delight, loss. Our loved ones, our work, our hobbies, our interests and life experiences are all described by how they make us feel.

There is a difference between feeling an emotion and being overwhelmed by it. When children become overwhelmed with emotion, their primitive brain takes over; they aim to survive which means less thinking and control over their bodies, feelings and actions.

It will take many years before your toddler will be able to regulate her emotions on her own.

Children learn about feelings from as early as nine months. At first your baby notices emotion by looking at your facial expressions and body language. He mirrors what you do. You smile and he smiles back; you love seeing him smile and you smile even more. And so you are having your first conversation with your baby. It starts off simple but over time develops into deeper, more complex interaction.

When both you and your child are calm and joyful, these little back-and-forth dances come easily. But there are so many times when they don't. We get hungry and tired, feel pressured and stressed out. Our primitive brain kicks in, takes over and blocks our thinking. Our behaviour becomes impulsive, unreasonable and inflexible.

Your toddler nagging you for another sweet at the end of a long day; your little girl having a meltdown over her favourite skirt being in the wash; or your child throwing himself on the ground kicking and screaming because he can't have the blue cup – these are the times when we, without thinking, use tactics such as:

- threats: "Stop whining or we're not going."
- shame: "Don't be such a baby!" or "You are such a whiner!"
- distraction: "It's not so bad. Look there … it's a birdie."
- reasoning: "There are no more sweets!"

Most of the time we rush in to stop the nagging, the whining and the meltdown, without doing what is most important: **acknowledging our child's feelings**. Even as adults the first thing we want from our spouses, partners and friends is for them to listen to what we are saying, loving and attentively.

If we feel understood and respected, we can move forward and start thinking about how to manage a situation.

Most of the time, we cannot control what emotions we are going to feel, when we feel them or how strongly we'll feel them. But we can control what we do with our feelings. Managing or controlling our emotions doesn't mean that we can't respond passionately, spontaneously, warmly and affectionately towards others and life experiences. It means **acknowledging** what we are feeling and **monitoring** our response to our emotions. "I'm feeling butterflies in my stomach. I'm slightly anxious. It's okay, I'm nearly there" or "I'm really upset now. Perhaps I need some time to regroup" or even "I'm really overreacting now. I need to stop immediately." In essence that is what defines **emotional regulation**.

> *We cannot control what emotions we are going to feel, when we'll feel them or how strongly we'll feel them. But we can control what we do with our feelings.*

# Feelings and regulation

Emotional regulation is being able to manage our emotions and express them in appropriate ways. The ability to regulate big feelings is essential for healthy development. It is a bit like driving a car and keeping to the speed limit. At times we need to apply the brakes and slow down the car, and at other times we can put our foot on the accelerator and speed up. We need to be able to experience a range of big feelings (the feel-good ones like joy and excitement, as well as the not-so-good ones like frustration, anger, anxiety and sadness), while staying calm and connected. But young children, with their immature brains, struggle to control bursts of powerful emotions. **Big emotions take over young brains and block their thinking.** Some of the big feelings that your toddler will experience:

## Children with good emotional regulation:

- Are able to experience, express and manage a wide range of emotions.
- Adjust well to transitions and new situations.
- Respond appropriately to emotional situations.
- Show a high tolerance for frustration.

## Children with poor emotional regulation:

- May exhibit a limited range of emotions.
- Have difficulties coping with stressful experiences.
- May engage in outbursts of negative emotions.
- May exhibit aggressive or egocentric behaviour (depending on their age).
- Are less socially competent, in general.
- Are often less successful in school – they find it difficult to learn, and are less productive in the classroom.

# Two critical reminders

## *How* you speak or *what* you say

Big feelings and learning in toddlers are like oil and water – they don't mix. If your child is upset, angry and agitated, his feeling brain will take over and he will not be able to absorb what you say and learn from it.

Because of the way his brain is wired, the right side that interprets *tone of voice* and *gestures* is far more active than the left side that understands *words*. This is even more evident when your child is experiencing big feelings. (No wonder they seem to have a hearing problem when they are upset!) *How you speak (and listen)* to your toddler is much more important than *what you say*. Just think about a time when you may have spilled your heart out to a friend and all she did was to carry on making the tea, while saying something like, "Oh dear", with an expressionless voice and a blank face. The same words would have meant so much more if your friend had touched your arm, looked you in the eye, raised her eyebrows and said them with feeling.

When you listen and speak to your toddler:

- bend down to his level;
- raise your eyebrows;
- nod your head while he is speaking; and
- use a few sounds or say a few brief words such as, "Mmm", "Wow!", "I see", "I hear you", "Oh no!", "Then what happened? " and "Tell me more". Your child's unique sensory temperament determines how much emotion you have to show.

- **Monkeys**, true to their nature, need more. They need us to show more of what we are feeling by using our voices, faces and bodies.
- **Giraffes** will also benefit from more volume, bigger movements and lots of facial expressions (at least until they are at the just right level of attentiveness).
- **Hedgehogs**, on the other hand, are very attuned to our non-verbal communication and the volume and pitch of our voices. Less is better for them as they can feel even more overwhelmed if we over-dramatise our feelings.

## Act as a container for your child's feelings

**Contain** your child's feelings. This does not mean putting the lid on and dismissing them, or letting the container overflow, which leads to complete dysregulation. Bear in mind that while we have to support our children and provide a container for their emotions, we do not need to do *all* the regulation for them *all* of the time. Neither should we attempt to make their world so comfortable that they never experience how it feels to make mistakes, or to be frustrated or worried. We live in such a quick-fix culture – we press a button and something happens – and there is a danger that we may expect the same when we parent. By jumping in, providing solutions and fixing everything, we deny our children the opportunity to learn self-regulation skills and living and experiencing life to the fullest. In fact, children need times when they feel anxious, frustrated or angry – *but* we must be available for them, providing the container. The milk does not disappear by being in a container. By being their container, we acknowledge our child's feelings (even if we don't think they are justified), we empathise and coach our child to come up with solutions to manage the feelings.

> **The goal of emotional regulation**
> *The goal of emotional regulation is for children to feel emotions, identify what they are feeling and then to choose appropriate ways of regulating those feelings.*

## Three steps to teach your child to regulate

We can help our children develop effective emotional regulation by teaching them to:
- become **aware** of the feelings
- **name** feelings by using words
- **express** feelings in an appropriate way.

Let's discuss each point individually and look at practical ways to implement the principles.

## 1 ) Help your child to become *aware* of feelings (identify)

Your toddler breaks one of her favourite toys and has a hissy fit. For the young toddler (under 24 months) it will be a good idea to make her aware of what she might be feeling by acting it out or demonstrating. Shake your head, stamp your feet, shrug your shoulders and droop your face – all the things that will convey her frustration, anger and regret. Remember: *what you say* is less important than *how you say it*.

Another way of helping children become aware of their big feelings is to make it visual and then talk about it. Fill balloons with water and throw them against a wall in the garden, then talk about how we sometimes feel like we are going to burst (with joy, with excitement or with frustration) just like the balloons. Or help him make a volcano (see below). This is a powerful way of demonstrating big feelings that want to bubble over, whether they are excitement, frustration, anger or fear. Describe the different stages of a volcano by relating it to what is happening in our bodies:

- too low/too slow – the volcano is inactive
- just right – the volcano is bubbling inside but is not overflowing and not dangerous to anybody
- too fast/too high – the volcano explodes and overflows.

Children find the words *bursting* and *exploding* really useful. When your child can say: "My body feels like it is going to explode", you can chill the champagne. It's time to celebrate – your child is becoming aware of how big feelings make him feel instead of just acting on them without considering the consequences.

**Making a volcano**

*What you need*

| | |
|---|---|
| 6 cups of flour | red food colouring |
| 2 cups salt | 6 drops of dishwashing liquid |
| 4 T cooking oil | 2 T baking soda |
| warm water | vinegar (just enough to slowly fill |
| empty plastic cooldrink bottle | the bottle) |
| baking dish or other pan | |

*Method*

1. Mix the flour, salt and oil with just enough warm water to make a smooth, firm mixture.
2. Stand the plastic bottle in the baking dish or pan and mould the dough around it into the shape of a mountain. Don't cover the hole at the top of the bottle or drop dough into it.
3. Fill the bottle almost to the top with warm water and a bit of red food colour.
4. Add the dishwashing liquid to the bottle. The detergent helps trap the bubbles produced by the reaction, which makes better lava.
5. Add the baking soda to the liquid in the bottle.
6. Slowly pour vinegar into the bottle. Watch out – eruption time!

## 2 ) Help your child *name* his feelings

As soon as your child can say that he feels angry, frustrated, jealous or excited, he is less likely to behave in challenging ways.

Children as young as two years old are able to learn the names of feelings. Let's use the example of your toddler who accidentally breaks her toy. You shrug your shoulders, you stamp your feet and you say: "You are feeling mad because your toy broke." Your child learns that the overwhelming feeling she experiences is one of anger.

A very important distinction that we need to make here is the fact that our children are separate from their behaviour. Their behaviour is not who they are. It is not that your child *is* mad. He is just *feeling* mad. It all lies in a very small word that carries lots of power. By saying: "I feel scared" rather than "I am scared" you are naming the emotion without becoming the emotion. The danger when we say *I am frustrated* rather than *I feel frustrated* lies in us becoming stuck in that behaviour. In doing so we are taking away opportunities for moving on, growing and trying new behaviours.

This is a very important distinction if we want to move onto the next step of regulating and choosing an appropriate way of expressing it.

You can practise this as follows:

- Use play with dolls or cars or animals and say things like: "The dolly is crying. She is feeling sad." or "The monkey is jumping up and down. He is feeling excited."
- Name-your-feelings games: When things are calm, play guessing games; make a happy face and ask your child if you look happy or sad, pull an angry face and ask her what you look like.
- Suggest phrases. Provide examples of phrases your child can effectively use in difficult situations, such as, "I was playing with that toy. Can I have it back?" or "After you, I would like a turn please." Practise these during times when things are calm or while playing pretend games with dolls and other toys.
- Use books and magazines. There are wonderful books for children of all ages that focus on dealing with emotions. These books offer opportunities to discuss emotions from a safe distance.
  - ◀ Find pictures in magazines of people with different facial expressions and paste them in a "feelings book". Ask your toddler to help you find them.
  - ◀ Read your favourite stories together, look at the emotions that the people and the animals are portraying and say, "Your rabbit looks sad. How do you look when you are sad?" or "How does that baby look to you: happy or sad?"

## 3 ) Help your child *express* his feelings

Children often fail to express their emotions in an appropriate way because they lack the vocabulary, they are dysregulated (perhaps in fight or flight) or they may feel afraid of expressing themselves. Here are some helpful tips and exercises to do when they are calm:

- Give permission to feel and express emotions. Children need to feel that it is okay to express all kinds of emotions – the positive and negative ones. Bottling up emotions leads to all kinds of problems, in the same way as expressing them in an inappropriate way does. It's all about the how. It's okay to feel frustrated, angry, sad and happy, but it's not okay to hit, bite, shout or scream.
- Use movement. Hit pillows, throw water balloons, stamp your feet while pretending to be elephants and say, "Sometimes when I'm angry my heart pumps fast. When I hit a pillow or stamp my feet I feel better. But I never ever hit somebody else."
- Use short phrases. The younger your toddler, the shorter your phrases should be. Instead of saying, "I can see you feel angry now, but we have to go, or we'll be late", rather just say, "Angry! You feel angry!"

I guarantee that the more you practise these steps, the sooner your child will start to develop successful self-regulation strategies so that he can acknowledge his feelings without becoming too overwhelmed by it or stuck in it.

**TIPS FOR INTENTIONAL PARENTS**

It is important to show our kids that we are vulnerable too. It is critical that we share some of our feelings, but we need to be intentional about how much we share and how often.

Saying that you are tired after a long day at work is enough, without going into all the details of the types of stresses you experienced throughout the day. Some children, especially the little **hedgehogs**, are overly sensitive to what you are feeling and may become anxious if you share too much intense emotion.

On the other hand, children who are under-responsive (**giraffes**) and over-responsive (**monkeys**) may need extra practice in developing empathy and benefit from more information.

Children of all temperaments will benefit from you being very specific about what you are feeling and why. Also use this time to demonstrate your own self-regulation strategies. You could say, "Mummy just needs a few minutes to slow down and recharge my batteries. I think I'm going to have a hot bath."

# 7

# Start thinking

......................................................

Piglet: 'Pooh?'
Pooh: 'Yes, Piglet?'
Piglet: 'I've been thinking …'
Pooh: 'That's a very good habit to get into to,
Piglet.'

– A.A. Milne, *Winnie-the-Pooh*

The most sophisticated part of the brain is the top front part, the thinking brain (the prefrontal cortex), which acts like its CEO. This is where everything comes together: we make decisions, solve problems and reflect on previous experiences, while considering other people's perspectives – highly complex reflective thinking skills. Research indicates that an assessment of these skills predicts success in life more accurately than traditional IQ tests. What better reason to help our children develop this part of their brain! Although it takes many years before the thinking brain is able to manage our behaviour and our emotions effectively, it is never too early to start.

## Why you need to switch on your child's thinking brain

> *"Well,"* said Pooh, *"what I like best,"* and then he had to stop and think. Because although eating honey was a very good thing to do, there was a moment just before you began to eat it which was better than when you were, but he didn't know what it was called.
>
> – A.A. Milne, *Winnie-the-Pooh*
>
> What I would like to say to Pooh is this:
> Dear Pooh, that moment you are referring to is when you are using your whole brain. You picture yourself eating honey, you remember what it is like to eat honey, and then you attach meaning and feelings to it. You could also say that *you are savouring the moment*. I agree it is a great thing to do and I like doing it too.

Strong connections in the thinking brain are essential for our wellbeing. And we can help our children form these. The more opportunities we give them to "get the juices flowing", the stronger the connections in their thinking brain will become. Use everyday interactions to get your child to train this part of his brain, then help him use his thinking to pull him through periods of dysregulation. Switching on your child's thinking brain will help him stay calm when the storms hit, grow up to be mature and have rich, meaningful experiences and relationships. His behaviour will no longer be determined solely by the primitive part of his brain.

## How to switch on your child's thinking brain

Each time your child stops and thinks – in other words, when he is not functioning on autopilot – his thinking brain will be switched on. Every time you say, "Convince me" or "What do you think will work for all of us?" you give him a chance to practise his thinking skills. With time and practice, your toddler will become aware of the consequences of his behaviour, and learn how to consider others. When you tell your toddler that it is time for his bath and he says, "No!" (something that happens at least a few times a day in any household with a toddler present), you can say, "You are saying no. Tell me why not. Give me a reason." Or, even better, "Give me three reasons why you don't want to bath now." The look in his eyes will tell you that you've managed to switch on his thinking brain, even though he may not be able to give you a fully formulated answer – yet.

# Activities to develop the thinking brain

There are loads of fun and interesting games that you can play with your child that will switch on and develop his thinking brain. Start early and you'll reap the benefits. Here are some examples:

- **Books** like *We're Going on a Bear Hunt* or *The Hungry Little Caterpillar* are great for teaching children to focus and pay attention, as well as get a sense of sequencing. Ask questions such as, "Where are we going next?" and "What are we going to do?"
- **Role playing.** Pretending to be a teacher, a mummy or the doctor provides opportunities for children to think, because they are behaving in ways that are different from how they naturally behave. This also increases their flexibility and empathy. Pretending that you are a baby and you aren't able to do anything for yourself is a good strategy when your toddler expects you to help him get dressed and you know very well that he is capable of doing it himself.
- **Pretend games.** Pretending that an object is something that it isn't is lots of fun. Pretend that the hairdryer is a microphone and have a karaoke session, a bowl can be a sunhat while you pretend to go to the beach, and a pencil can be a comb while playing hairdresser.
- **I spy games.** "I spy with my little eye something that is red", "I spy something beginning with A", "I spy something that rhymes with *floor*".
- **I-went-shopping games.** "I went shopping and I bought … a loaf of bread, a green apple, a litre of milk and a bag of potatoes". Each player repeats the sequence from the beginning and adds another item. This is a great game to play in the car or while waiting in a queue, especially with two or more children.
- **Idea pool.** Ask your older toddler (twenty-four months and up) to come up with as many ideas as possible for different things to do with an ordinary object. For example, a scarf can become a hat, a skipping rope, a measuring tape, a blindfold and a line to jump over or to walk on like a balancing beam. Encourage your child to come up with as many options as she can, even if most of them aren't practical.
- **Wrong-word games.** The idea behind this game is to sabotage the "autopilot" and put a twist on words that gets the thinking brain going. It is usually very popular with kids and works well as soon as children are able to distinguish between what's real and what isn't (usually from the age of four years, but in some children even earlier). There is no rule for this game except that everything is wrong. For example, ask "Do you want the blue cup?" when you are actually holding the pink cup in your hands; "Eat with the shovel please", when you are handing your toddler a spoon; say, "no" when you mean "yes" and "yes" when you mean "no"; "Let's dry you before you get into the bath", when you actually dry your child *after* getting *out* of the bath; "I really don't like getting cuddles from you", when you love cuddles.
- **Upside-down games.** Board games could be adapted, for instance snakes take the counter up while ladders take it down. This is great fun and the opportunities are endless. You can even play Simon-says, but the goal is for the children to do the opposite of what you are telling them to do. For example, if you say, "Simon says … stand up", the children should sit down, or when you say, "Simon says … rub your tummy", they should rub their backs.
- **The "Why?" game.** Toddlers love asking "Why?" and it is important that we try to answer their questions. But to get them really thinking, it's also good to throw the *whys* back at them. Answer your toddler's "Why?" in response to a request from you with, "Why do *you* think that

is?" When playing with your toddler ask, "Why is your baby crying?" or "Why is that bridge you've built so high?" Even if you initially have to answer the questions yourself, you will stimulate your child to think in this sophisticated way. It is amazing how long you can keep a conversation going by asking, "Why?" The other day we managed a hundred "Why?" questions between my youngest daughter and me. We didn't stop because we were running out of answers. We simply stopped because, as she described it, "Our brains felt roasted and we both got a bit bored and tired of the game."

- **The "What?" game.** When your toddler asks, "What is that, Mummy?" answer him by asking, "What do *you* think that is?" Obviously we shouldn't do this every time our children ask us questions, but at times it is a good way of getting the thinking juices flowing. You can guide him and give him clues: "Do you think it is a …? " starting with very clearly wrong answers.
- **The "What if?" game.** Playing this is great for several reasons. Children of any age (from a toddler with a vocabulary of only a few words to older toddlers) can play and you can play it anywhere – in the car, in a queue, in a waiting room, around the dining table. Combine real-life scenarios with pretend ones, and extraordinary ideas with ordinary – it's great fun! Ask questions such as, "What would happen if … we got lost in the jungle with slithering snakes and roaring tigers … what would we do?" or "What if … we walk along the road and we see an ant? What if the ant suddenly grows and becomes as big as you? Maybe it's all the colours of the rainbow instead of black. What if the ant starts speaking to us? What would he say?" The "What if?" game gets the thinking brain fired up, so it is great to use at the moment just before your toddler hits meltdown or has a tantrum. For example, you tell your toddler that it is time to get out of the bath and he starts complaining. Ask, "What would happen if we stayed in the bath *all* night?"

Your toddler's thinking brain takes time and lots of practice to develop. But, remember, the brain is like a muscle – the more you exercise it, the stronger it becomes.

# PART III

............................................

# Facing challenges

# Challenging behaviour

·····································································

*"I'm not lost for I know where I am. But however, where I am may be lost."*

– A.A. Milne, *Winnie-the-Pooh*

Every parent's nightmare … The teacher calls you in and says that your child has bitten another child; the yelling, screaming and kicking in the shop when you said "no"; the sibling rivalry that gets out of control; the play date that consists of your child snatching away everything his playmate touches; the crying that doesn't stop if you leave him for a second; the sitting on your lap throughout the party, refusing to join in the fun.

Let's face it, the hardest part of parenting is when your child's behaviour becomes challenging. Sure, there was the sleep deprivation of the first year and the worries surrounding feeding, but nobody can prepare you for the day when your toddler has her first full-blown temper tantrum in a public place. You may have been taken aback when the first hissy fit happened at home, but, after you overcame the shock at the sudden change in your toddler's personality, you made yourself a cup of tea and calculated how long it would be until she turned two (because she is only eighteen months and they say it gets worse at two). But when it happened in the busy supermarket, the blood rushed to your face, your heart skipped several beats and your palms started to sweat. It's a humbling experience – the temper tantrum – at least with your first child and for the first few times.

# What is your child trying to tell you?

It gets my blood boiling when I hear children being labelled as "the naughty one", "the biter" or "the bully". Children aren't born that way – they don't have a gene that causes them to be *the naughty one*. In general there will be a valid reason or several reasons *why* children behave the way they do. Your child is trying to tell you something by behaving in certain ways. Finding reasons for his challenging behaviour, whatever it might be, may be an uncomfortable process. But it is important – for him and for you. Your efforts at trying to make sense of the *whys* will not only bear fruit in the long run; they are also vitally important if you want to raise an emotionally and socially healthy child.

## What is challenging behaviour?

Challenging behaviour, and its frequency and the intensity, differs from child to child. It includes:
- Moodiness
- Meltdowns
- Withdrawal
- Fears, anxiety and stress
- Hyperactivity
- Temper tantrums (which range from whining to screaming and breath holding)
- Aggressive behaviour such as biting, hitting, kicking and bullying
- Destructive behaviour such as breaking and throwing things, head banging or self-injury

## Why does challenging behaviour occur?

Challenging behaviour occurs because something is not quite right – something is out of balance. Dysregulation causes challenging behaviour and challenging behaviour causes further dysregulation. It is a bit like a domino effect or a spiral that goes round and round and round. Getting to the bottom of it and interpreting the behaviour is key in breaking this cycle. Children who are dysregulated – whether it is due to trauma, sensory overload, developmental difficulties or environmental stressors – often behave in challenging ways.

The word "challenging" tends to evoke negative feelings that can result in antagonism towards and frustration with our child. Some experts suggest rephrasing "challenging" behaviour as "stressed" behaviour (especially in children under five). When you do that, challenging behaviour suddenly takes on another meaning. It makes it easier for us to empathise with the child and ask questions such as, "Why do you feel that way?" and "What can I do to make you feel less worried?"

The *why* and the *what* are important. Behaviour is a form of communication. When your child is having a meltdown or a temper tantrum or is starting to withdraw, she is trying to tell you something. Finding appropriate ways to deal with challenging behaviours, necessitates a look beyond the behaviour. We need to ask ourselves, "Why is my child demonstrating this challenging behaviour?"

# Common reasons for challenging behaviour

Let's look at some common reasons why children, specifically those under the age of five, challenge us with their behaviour. We will discuss:
- Tiredness
- Hunger
- A young, not fully developed brain
- Sensory temperament challenges
- Lack of structure and boundaries
- Disconnectedness within the parent-child relationship

## Tiredness

We all know what a good night's sleep does for us: it makes us feel refreshed, and able to concentrate and deal with life's challenges in a productive and calm manner. But when we are sleep deprived, we become moody, easily frustrated, unproductive and unfocused. Those early years – when babies require night feeds and we are trying to establish sleep patterns – can be one of the most challenging times in a parent's life. The same principle applies to our kids – **children who get enough sleep are more likely to function better and are less prone to behaviour problems and moodiness**. When children sleep, the natural calming systems of the body are topped up. This stabilises their mood and promotes their ability to self-regulate, enabling them to stay calm and attentive. During sleep, their brains shift the information learnt during the day to more efficient storage regions in the brain. So, the more the child has experienced during the day, the more he needs to sleep that night.

### LACK OF SLEEP
This causes the stress system in the brain to be in the driving seat – which results in challenging behaviour, moodiness, meltdowns, tantrums, kicking, screaming and generally dysregulated behaviour. With continuous lack of sleep, the effect on a child's regulating systems can be even more devastating, causing imbalances in blood-sugar levels, and mood changes including aggression, anxiety and depression. The part of the brain that suffers most is the thinking brain – the part that is responsible for impulse control, decision-making, paying attention, staying calm and learning.

Surprisingly, sleep-deprived children don't always look sleepy during the day. They are often overactive and disruptive. You've all experienced a child who has gone past his bedtime hour – they seem wide awake and are often "hyper" or "uncontrollable". Even a giraffe (a child who is generally under-responsive) can suddenly change into a monkey and exhibit behaviour such as impulsiveness and hyperactivity. This change in behaviour is easy to explain. An overtired child's body will fight the fatigue by releasing adrenaline – the hormone that gets us going – in an effort to keep him awake. Adrenaline released at inappropriate times will result in dysregulation – too much go and too little slow. Not only will the child be overactive, but his ability to calm himself and organise his behaviour is also decreased.

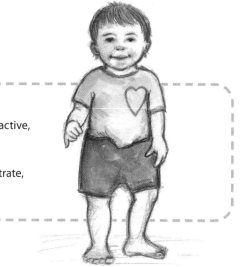

**Lack of sleep affects a child on all levels**
- Behaviour – impulsive, overactive, hyperactive, silly, tired
- Mood – cranky, irritable, frustrated
- Thinking – inattentive, unable to concentrate, make decisions or solve problems

## HEALTHY SLEEP PATTERNS

These are dependent on and affected by your child's physical age, her emotional age, her sensory temperament and her ability to regulate. Factors such as her health, eating habits, routines and schedules, the sleep environment, her daytime activities, and your ability to read and respond to her cues all contribute to the establishment of healthy sleep patterns.

Most sleep experts agree on the following:

- Daytime sleeps are essential for babies and toddlers and directly affect how well they sleep at night.
- Daytime stimulation (whether it is physical, intellectual or emotional) will also affect how well your child sleeps at night. Children who have had to deal with lots of anxiety and stress during the day or who suffered from a meltdown or a tantrum (especially during the late afternoon) could end up having disrupted sleep.
- Around the world, children get an hour less sleep than they did thirty years ago. Recent research has confirmed that chronic poor sleep results in daytime tiredness, lack of focus, irritability and frustration, impulsiveness, moodiness and obesity. As Alan Greene says: "These are the same symptoms that can earn kids the diagnosis of … attention deficit hyperactivity disorder (ADHD)." Research in sleep laboratories has revealed that some kids are mislabelled with ADHD when the real problem is chronic, partial sleep deprivation.

## Hunger

This is another factor that can turn children into little monsters. Your child's body and brain are continually engaged in a complex physiological process that includes stabilising blood-sugar levels and balancing hormones. When your child has been without food for too long, his blood-sugar level falls and his body will respond by releasing stress hormones (cortisol and adrenaline), because they are designed to raise blood-sugar levels. This peaking and falling of blood-sugar levels results in moodiness, hyperactive behaviour and a decrease in attention and concentration.

When I'm battling to get the kids downstairs for breakfast I often say, "I'm so hungry, if I don't get food *now*, I will turn into an ogre!" (An extremely irritable and tend-to-sweat-the-small-stuff ogre!)

Swings in blood-sugar levels – the "spike-and-crash syndrome" – are triggered by:

- not having breakfast
- eating sugar (sweets and chocolates) on an empty stomach
- food additives (the E additives in foods, especially junk food and fizzy drinks).

To keep up with this fast-paced life, parents and children need food that **sustains energy** and **stabilises moods**.

**Stable blood-sugar levels** are important for a balanced brain and body. The glycemic index (GI) of food should be borne in mind when selecting food. All types of food have an effect on the blood-sugar level in your body – carbohydrates have a direct effect, while proteins and fats have a more indirect effect. Some carbohydrates take longer to digest and are called low-GI foods, while others, the high-GI foods, are digested very quickly, leaving the body with limited fuel and in an unbalanced state.

**Low-GI foods** will provide the body with fuel and make us feel full for approximately three hours. They give us stamina or staying power. High-GI foods fuel the body only for about an hour and can cause a slump in mood (irritability) and in energy levels (which often causes children to look hyper, as their bodies are desperately trying to restore the balance). The goal is to keep your child's (and your!) blood-sugar levels as stable as possible during the day, resulting in stable moods and sustained energy for most of the day. There is one exception to the rule – providing the body with high-GI food after exercise (ten to thirty minutes afterwards) will replace depleted energy stores and increase the body's ability to heal.

## A young, not fully developed brain

Your baby is born with an amazing brain that is able to take in information from his senses and regulate basic functions such as breathing, pumping blood through the body, body temperature and digestion. However, most of your baby's brain will continue to develop after birth (in fact, ninety per cent of the development takes place after birth, with the thinking part of the brain being the last to develop). As we saw in Chapter 2, your child's brain is still under construction. Children under five years are driven by their big emotions; the thinking part of the brain, which is responsible for logical thinking and problem-solving, is still very immature and undeveloped. This means that they are simply not able to control their impulses and calm themselves at all times by using thoughts and problem-solving without your help. There will be times when your child might amaze you. Today she may manage to walk away and find another toy after her friend snatched the one she was playing with, but tomorrow she may have a full-blown meltdown when the same thing happens. As your child develops and matures, she will develop the ability to self-regulate, provided you parent these skills intentionally. An increase in the ability to self-regulate means a decrease in challenging behaviour.

It is important to understand that a baby between birth and twelve months cannot deliberately be "naughty" or defiant, or test the boundaries or manipulate you. Your baby may laugh if you tell him, "No!", when he tries to put his finger in the electric socket or when he spits out his food, because his brain is not developed enough to interpret the meanings of discipline and establishing rules. Between the ages of one and two years, your toddler learns what it means if you raise your voice, pull a stern face or point your finger at him to warn or reprimand him. The glutamate system, a chemical system in the thinking brain, guides our intentions and thoughts – including destructive ones such as manipulation and rudeness. This system is not yet properly established in the first year of life. A baby under a year does not have the intellectual capacity to be deliberately rude, manipulative and defiant.

## Challenges related to sensory temperament

Children's temperaments vary dramatically; while some may regularly behave in challenging ways, others rarely do. Remember the fuel tank analogy? Sensory input is the fuel that we use to fill up the tank. A tank that is overflowing causes dysregulation, which will most likely result in some sort of challenging behaviour.

- **Giraffes** have big tanks, and it takes a considerable amount of fuel to fill them. Children who have large tanks will be less likely to behave in challenging ways, since they don't easily become overloaded.
- **Hedgehogs** have small tanks that, with only a little bit of extra fuel, will overflow. Sensory-sensitive children have heightened alarm systems, which means that they are easily pushed into a state of fight or flight. They tend to over-respond to sights, sounds, movement and pain that are part of everyday life. All of this makes them more inclined to feeling anxious and fearful, and having meltdowns.
- **Monkeys** have huge tanks but gas guzzling engines. They need heaps of sensory input to keep functioning optimally. Sensory cravers have a heightened drive for movement and touch and, when these aren't met, they become dysregulated. Monkeys' challenging behaviour includes rages, aggression, anger and meltdowns.

## Lack of structure and boundaries

All humans have a psychological need for structure. Unstructured days are the ones that often make me feel less energised, less focused and a little depressed. The same applies to children – especially toddlers with developing brains. They are not yet able to come up with their own rules and routines without our help. Children feel safe in an environment structured by consistent routines and clear, age-appropriate boundaries. They are calmer because they know what is expected of them. Both experience and science tell us that environments without the containment of boundaries and routines are the breeding ground of challenging behaviours.

## Disconnectedness within the parent–child relationship

The bond or attachment that children form with their parents and/or a consistent caregiver is fundamental to their development. Children perceive their bonds with parents to be strong and secure if the parent is available and responsive when needed. Strong bonds and connectedness provide a base from which the child is able to explore her environment and manage stress. Children who feel connected with their parents are more cooperative and behave in less challenging ways.

Be intentional about nurturing the connection with your child, especially during challenging times.

- Be intentionally warm and responsive.
- Meet your child at his level, go down on your knees and look him in the eye when he's talking to you. Be intentional and make hellos and goodbyes moments of connection, with you always crouching down to his level.
- Be spontaneous in giving her lots of cuddles and hugs.

- Be deliberate about sharing time, doing calm activities like snuggling up on his bed and reading him a story.
- Engage in rough-and-tumble play, look for the humour in your day and share moments of laughter and fun.
- Get onto the floor with your child and play with her. Let her be the leader and the boss. Make your playtime child-led rather than parent-dominated.

# Fears, anxieties and stress

............................................................

*Piglet sidled up to Pooh from behind. "Pooh?"*
*he whispered.*
*"Yes, Piglet?"*
*"Nothing," said Piglet, taking Pooh's hand.*
*"I just wanted to be sure of you."*
— A.A. Milne, *Winnie-the-Pooh*

Our child's brain and body react to fears, anxiety and stress as much as ours do. As human beings, we are created to deal with short spurts of stress and anxiety, but when the stress or anxiety is long-lasting it interferes with development and can be harmful and unhealthy.

If children are fearful or feel anxious, the consequence is a brain and body that are out of balance – dysregulated – even if the fear or angst is only for a brief second. Consistently being warm, attentive (keeping the relationship as the priority) as well as deliberate in providing age-appropriate controllable challenges is crucial in helping to shape your child's brain and restoring balance.

The goal is that, over time, your child should develop the ability to manage his fears, anxieties and stress effectively.

# Fear, anxieties and stress take over

Fears, anxieties and stress have a way of taking over. If not contained, they will spread and become nearly impossible to avoid. They are like a litre of spilt milk – without a container it will spread out and run everywhere. Changes and transitions contribute to feelings of fear, anxiety and stress in children, especially for our sensitive children, the hedgehogs.

The beginning of a new school year was approaching. I noticed towards the end of the holiday that something wasn't quite right. My daughter's behaviour was out of character. She seemed frazzled and confused, and I found myself having to repeat normal everyday things over and over again. She bombarded me with questions about our plans for the day, when we were going to do what, how this would work and how we'd do that – often asking me more than once. Her problem-solving ability decreased – she couldn't lay the table or work out what to do when we ran out of toothpaste. She broke down in floods of tears over trivial things, her frustration level was low and meltdowns were frequent. She was being impulsive and made hurtful comments to family members, which were followed by severe regret and guilt.

At the end of the first day back at school, when I asked her what homework she had, she said she couldn't remember. She told me that she felt as if her heart was racing in class, and the sound of her heart beating was blocking out her teacher's voice. On a few occasions she had physical complaints, such as headaches, dizziness, nausea, difficulty breathing and blurred vision. I saw a little girl with tightly rounded shoulders who seemed desperate to curl up into a little ball – just like a hedgehog. It was clear to me that her fears and anxiety about the new school year were causing out-of-sorts behaviour and severe dysregulation, affecting her ability to learn and function in this busy world. She was like that litre of spilt milk, and desperately needed a container.

Like adults, children often have big feelings and difficulty handling their stress. When your child is overwhelmed – whether by something internal like being hungry or external like danger, harm or fear (real or imaginary) – his body will tell him. His brain senses that something is wrong and activates the alarm system, which in turn helps the body get what it needs. As your child matures, so does his ability to manage his fears, anxiety and stress. The neighbours' dog's barking might have given him a real fright when he was a year old, but now, at four years old, he hardly seems to notice it. Over time his brain has been conveying the message that the barking is okay and will not cause him any harm.

Your child's developing body and brain are highly vulnerable to stress. Unfortunately some common parenting techniques do not help children to deal effectively with the stress that they experience. Let me spell these out: *parenting techniques such as "the naughty step", "crying it out" and punishing (including smacking) do not work when you are dealing with children who are fearful, anxious and stressed out.* They might work in the moment – your child will stop crying if you threaten him with the naughty step. However, this separation-based discipline and punishment will not help your child in the long run. Brain-imaging studies reveal that these discipline methods, especially when you're dealing with a sensitive and anxious child, result in permanent changes in the child's brain and, in severe cases, mental disorders and physical ailments.

> *"There is a mass of scientific research showing that quality of life is dramatically affected by whether or not you established good stress-regulating systems in your brain in childhood."* Margot Sunderland

So what do we do then? How can we be sure that our parenting will not cause any long-term damage in our children? The answer lies in this: *we have to be very aware, thoughtful and deliberate about helping our children establish effective stress-regulating strategies.* **We cannot prevent our children from experiencing fears, anxieties and stress in life, but we can influence their response.**

✓ When a child is not given enough help early in his life in managing his feelings of fear and anxiety, his brain will not develop the essential pathways for effective stress management later in life.

Experts agree that adults that were nurtured and helped to develop self-calming and stress-management strategies when they were children are better able to deal with stress than adults who haven't been nurtured and coached.

# How fear, anxiety and stress affect children

Imagine you're in the traffic … stuck on the highway and late for an important appointment. Then someone cuts you off … You feel as if you want to explode. You have to use every ounce of emotional and physical energy you can master to control yourself. That rush of intense feelings was triggered in a little almond-shaped structure in your emotional brain – the amygdala. The amygdala acts like the watchdog for our brain and allows us to act before we think – important for the times when you have to jump out of the road to avoid a speeding driver. It can take over the rest of the brain in an instant, enabling us to act quickly. This is called an *amygdala hijack*. The problem with this hijacking system is that the amygdala often gets it wrong. In a sense you can say that it overreacts. It interprets only a fraction of the information coming in from the eye and ear. Most of the information goes to other parts of the brain that take longer to process, analyse and interpret. As soon as the information reaches the thinking brain, it calms the amygdala. *Children under five with undeveloped thinking brains are most at risk of the amygdala hijack*. All attention is on the stressor and your child will not be able to learn and think clearly. Activating your child's thinking brain will instantly calm him, because it overrides the effects from the amygdala. Your three-year-old who has a screaming fit when you tell him that he is not allowed another yoghurt needs your help. Pick him up, show him something else that will get him thinking, do something silly to make him laugh. Activate his thinking brain and calm his rage. Once he is calm he might be more able to reason with you and understand why you are saying no to another yoghurt.

# Reasons for fear, anxiety and stress in children

There are several reasons why children might start worrying and why they become anxious. Some of the main reasons are:
- Typical anxieties related to your child's emotional developmental age. These include fear of being left alone, fear of the dark and fear of loud noises. See the table on page 110 for more information.
- Growth spurts, hormonal changes, allergies, illness, poor nutrition, and lack of sleep and/or exercise are also contributors to stress and anxiety.
- Unresolved or undetected medical conditions such as ear infections, constipation and allergies can cause stress and anxieties.
- Hedgehogs – children with a sensory-sensitive temperament – have a low threshold and can easily become overloaded. Loud noises, overcrowding, scratchy clothing and lumpy food switch on the alarm system in the brain, which results in fears, anxiety and stress.
- Developmental delays and other sensory processing difficulties can cause stress and anxiety. These include delays in language acquisition, poor comprehension, difficulties with visual–spatial processing and motor planning.

# Typical anxieties in children

Typical childhood anxieties start when a child has developed a certain understanding about his world. Your child only really starts having fears about things like monsters in her bedroom that keep her from falling asleep if she is able to link the fear to a concept. This usually happens between three and four years of age.

**FEARS AND ANXIETIES FOLLOW A DEVELOPMENTAL PATTERN**

| Age | Developmentally determined fear and anxiety |
|---|---|
| Within first few weeks | Fear of loss, e.g. physical contact with caregivers |
| 0–6 months | Fear of significant sensory stimuli that cause a fight-or-flight response, e.g. dog barking, door slamming, or any sudden, loud noise |
| 6–8 months | Shyness/anxiety with strangers |
| 12–18 months | Separation anxiety often causing sleep disturbances, severe stubbornness and anger (oppositional defiant behaviour) |
| 2–3 years | Fear of thunder and lightning, fire, water, darkness; nightmares resulting in crying, clinging, withdrawal, freezing, seeking security and physical contact, night terrors, bed-wetting (after being potty-trained) |
| 4–5 years | Fear of death or dead people |
| 5–7 years | Fear becomes much more specific due to the emotional and brain development that becomes more complex; it includes fear of specific objects (animals or monsters), fear of germs and getting ill, fear of natural disasters or a fear of a traumatic event (being hit by a car) |
| 8 years and up | Social and performance anxieties result in not wanting to go to school, withdrawal, timidity, extreme shyness and feelings of shame |
| 12–18 years | Fear of rejection by peers |

# Separation anxiety

Separation anxiety is a typical childhood anxiety and part of growing up. It is highly likely that at some point your child will experience some separation anxiety, but how much and for how long varies from child to child. What brings children out of this anxiety is the ability to form a concept of space and time, e.g. "Mummy will be back later to pick me up", which indicates an activation of the thinking part of the brain.

Sensitive children (hedgehogs) tend to experience separation anxiety more intensely owing to the already heightened alarm system in their brains.

Our society and culture is driven towards separating our children from their mothers at an earlier and earlier age. Our children are put in cots and left to cry, they stay in car seats and prams for long hours during the day and we drop them at childcare centres from an early age. The reality is that we all lead very busy lives and, in all fairness, most parents don't employ nannies or drop their children at crèches without careful consideration. However, there is growing concern among developmental specialists about the general lack of understanding of the effect of unsupportive parenting on our children's brains. Risks include regulation disorders, behavioural problems, anxiety disorders, depression and the breakdown of parent–child relationships.

### WHY DOES MY CHILD CLING TO ME?

Some children latch onto their parents when they find it hard to separate. It is important to recognise that, if your child does this, it is not because he wants to irritate you or cause a scene. He is simply acting on a very primitive response that is triggered without rational thought – the need for physical touch when we are stressed, in an effort to calm the brain and body. We seldom see teenagers still clinging onto their parents at the school gates. I can assure you that your child will grow and develop, and as he matures the thinking part of his brain will temper the primitive parts of his brain that become overly sensitive through separation. It is important to find ways of dealing with separation anxiety and clinginess, so that your child is able to separate while feeling secure and calm.

## SEPARATION ANXIETY AND YOUR CHILD'S BRAIN

High levels of cortisol, a stress hormone, are not experienced only by children who cry when left with the nanny, at the playgroup or at school. Some children don't cry, but may still experience equally high levels of stress hormones. When your child is anxious owing to the separation, it increases the release of cortisol in his brain.

- Cortisol levels rise and fall naturally during the day, being highest in the morning.
- Cortisol levels that stay high cause hypersensitivity, stress and depression later in life.
- Cortisol levels are brought down and balanced through holding, soothing and distraction from the source of anxiety.

**HOW TO MAKE SEPARATION EASY FOR YOU AND YOUR CHILD**

One thing is certain: you will leave your child with somebody at some point, whether it is with the nanny, granny or at crèche. This six-step plan will ensure healthy separation for healthy emotional development.

- **Play separation games in a reassuring and fun way,** such as peek-a-boo, walking out of the room while talking and then coming back, or crawling through a tunnel – anything that makes you disappear and then appear again.
- **Practise separation at home** for brief periods by leaving your child with a very familiar friend or family member in your own home.
- **Have quality time shortly before the separation** as this will increase the release of feel-good hormones in your child's brain and make him calmer.
- **Ensure that the person who will be looking after your child is warm and loving at all times,** able to share your child's joy and excitement by matching his facial expressions and tone of voice, and able to support and care when he is showing signs of distress by physical touch (holding and cuddling, putting your child on her lap, sitting next to him and talking to him in a calm, soothing voice).
- **Use distraction** with a toy or game that interests your child. This will activate the thinking part of her brain and decrease the stress response. Sensory play has been known to do wonders in terms of calming; this includes water play, sand play, play dough and textured play (e.g. sensory boxes as described on page 20).
- **Use a tactile and or visual object that reminds your child of you** when he continues to be distressed by separation. Your child might have difficulties with concepts of space, time and people. He will benefit from having access to a scarf that smells like you, a photo of you and a visual chart that indicates the routine of the day and when it is time for him to be picked up.

**DO NOT**

- Rush off or attempt a quick escape when your child is not looking. Although this makes it easier for you because you don't have to deal with a crying or screaming child, your child will experience a rush of stress hormones and chemicals that could last between twenty and forty minutes before her body and brain reach a balanced state again. Not great, especially if the goal is to teach our children the ability to regulate emotions of fear and anxiety.
- Give negative feedback such as "Don't cry, you are not a baby." Children who suffer from separation anxiety need your calm and attentive help, not judgemental comments that dismiss their big feelings, leaving them feeling helpless and shamed.

**Loving touch**
Well-known research on infant rhesus monkeys that were left without their mothers revealed that the little monkeys went to a wire mesh body, which provided milk, only when they were hungry. They spent the rest of the time clinging to a soft, cloth-covered surrogate body. Don't underestimate the effects of loving touch!

### RED FLAGS FOR ANXIETY SEPARATION DISORDER IN CHILDREN

Some children experience separation anxiety that doesn't go away, even with the parents' best efforts. If separation anxiety is excessive enough to interfere with normal activities like school and friendships, and lasts for months rather than days, it may be a sign of a bigger problem that includes difficulty forming a mental picture of Mummy (difficulties with visual–spatial thinking), and/or difficulty with forming a secure attachment.

If you see any of the following "red flags" and your interventions don't seem to be enough, it may be necessary to get a professional to diagnose and help your child with separation anxiety disorder.

- Age-inappropriate clinginess or tantrums
- Constant complaints of physical sickness
- Withdrawal from friends, family or peers
- Refusal to go to school for weeks
- Preoccupation with intense fear or guilt
- Excessive fear of leaving the house

**WHAT RESEARCH TELLS US ABOUT STRESS MANAGEMENT**

Stress management is learnt during critical periods early in life. Babies and children who receive gentle handling are better able to cope with stress and have stronger immune systems. As John Ratey explains in his book, *A User's Guide to the Brain*, research on newborn rats (which have brain neurons very similar to humans) indicates that the more gently the rats are handled, the more they produce serotonin, a brain chemical that controls aggressive behaviour. As adults, the rats that had received gentle handling were better able to cope with stress, had stronger immune systems, and actually lived longer than rats that had not been treated gently.

# How to de-stress your child

As you might have discovered already, simply telling a fearful or anxious child to stop worrying doesn't help. We need to deal with this in an intentional way with the long-term goal to establish effective stress management skills.

## Address your own stress and anxiety first

It is inevitable that at some stage we will be burdened with worries, stress and fears, and we might feel exhausted, irritable, frustrated and overwhelmed. We need to be aware of our own levels of anxiety and the effects of stress. Look after yourself, be real about your feelings and ask for help if you need to. Ask your family and friends or professionals to support you and reduce your feelings of stress and anxiety. Our children need us to be as available and as regulated as we possibly can be. There will be times when we lose control, and that is not a bad thing. During these times there are valuable lessons to be learnt. However, long-lasting anxiety and stress will have devastating effects on your health and your relationship with your child.

# Help your toddler deal with fears, anxiety and stress

## Sort out the basics

Setting up a good routine at home and ensuring that your child is eating a nutritious, low-GI diet and getting enough sleep and exercise are part of getting your child's body and brain balanced. If you suspect that your child may have any underlying, undiagnosed medical issues, such as untreated ear infections and allergies, a visit to a paediatrician is recommended.

## Provide loving touch

Lovingly touching your child activates the release of anti-stress chemicals in his brain, which will leave him feeling calm and regulated. Fun touch games and interactions that you can try at home:

- Blow "raspberries" on his tummy.
- Lower your body and your voice, take your child's hands in yours and make loving eye contact with every hello and goodbye.
- Play row-row-row your boat.
- Sit your child on your lap, give her a cuddle and read a story.
- Scoop your child up in your arms and pretend that you are going to eat his nose, ears, finger.
- Dance with your child, throw her in the air and tilt her upside down and throw her over your shoulder.

> *"The more warm, unconditional, constant, and physically affectionate your relationship is with your child, the stronger the release of opioids, oxytocin, and prolactin (anti-stress hormones) in his brain."*
> Margot Sunderland

## Create opportunities for deep-pressure touch

Touch that is not light and fluffy but is deep and sustained is organising and calming. Fun games to try at home:

- Give your child big bear hugs.
- Squash her between pillows.
- Roll him up tightly in a blanket or duvet (hot-dog game).
- Massage your child.
- Put him in a tight-fitting all-in-one swimsuit (two sizes too small) for a while during the day.
- Give your child a warm bath with calming essential oils such as camomile or lavender.

## Provide opportunities for heavy work

Activities that involve pulling, pushing, crashing and lifting are organising and calming.
Fun games to try at home:
• Wheelbarrow walks.
• Animal walks – pretending to be an elephant and taking big noisy footsteps, crawling like a snake, walking on hands and feet sideways like a crab.
• Encourage your child to wear small, light wrist and/or ankle weights for short periods of time.
• Push-ups.
• Having your child make a bridge by lying on her back, with her legs bent, and pushing her bottom up in the air until the front of her body is completely flat.
• Playing tug-of-war with your child – place the palms of your hands against your child's palms and push against each other, then lock your hands and pull away from each other.
• Chewing gum for older children, sucking yoghurt through a straw.

## Teach proper breathing

Teaching children to breathe deeply gives them a powerful tool to reduce the physical symptoms of stress and anxiety. But children often find it difficult to grasp the concept of "breathe deeply in and out", as we would instruct adults to do. Therefore it is helpful to focus on breathing out first, because a full exhalation will automatically be followed up by a deep inhalation. The following techniques will be helpful in teaching your child proper breathing:
• Put a flimsy, transparent scarf on your child's face and get her to blow it up in the air or even off her face.
• Blow a tissue or feather in the air and then attempt to keep it there for as long as possible.
• Blow up a balloon.
• Blow bubbles with commercially available bubbles.
• Play blowing races or blowing football – use a straw and a ball of cotton wool or a table-tennis ball in a big bowl of water.
• Encourage an older child to put his hands on his tummy and, when he is breathing in, pretend that he is blowing up a balloon (his tummy must rise up and outwards); when he breathes out, the balloon deflates.

## Spend time playing

Playing with your child on the floor – following his lead, letting him be in control, doing the things and playing the games that he finds enjoyable – will release the anti-stress chemicals that in turn will reduce stress and anxiety. Smile and laugh when you play with your child. Your child will mirror your smiling and laughing, which in turn can help decrease the levels of stress-enhancing hormones (cortisol and adrenaline) and increase the levels of mood-enhancing hormones (endorphins).

## Help him deal with *big feelings*

As a toddler your child will begin to experience feelings like pride, shame, guilt, embarrassment, excitement, joy, anger and frustration – all for the first time. We need to help our children to navigate through the tides of strong emotions so that they don't get too overwhelmed by them. Through playing and interacting with our children we encourage them to become aware of what they are feeling, to give names to their feelings and then to express them without becoming overwhelmed.

### BACH FLOWER REMEDIES

From past experience, I believe that children respond well to Bach Flower Remedies. A consultation with a specialist at a health store is recommended before choosing which one(s) to use. A few drops in their juice will make a difference, especially when used over a period of time. For acute stress and anxiety Rescue Remedy, which comes in drops, sucking drops, tablets and cream, is a good addition to your medicine cabinet.

### Learn from the meerkats

I recently witnessed how a troop of meerkats cope with the acute stress that is part of an animal's life. They live in large family groups and work together to solve problems and survive. This family's territory was invaded by a rival troop while they were out searching for food. On their return, they saw what was happening and each of them demonstrated typical stress behaviour: they stood up tall, noses in the air, and looked around frantically ... you could sense the tension in the air. They made fast, vigorous movements – all driven by the stress hormones adrenaline and cortisol. They seemed revved up and within seconds scurried towards the rivals at full speed. The rivals were caught off guard and retreated immediately. They cuddled, they played, they climbed over and under each other, they rolled back and forth – they used their bodies and lots of playful interactions and physical closeness to bring their brains and bodies back into balance. Within a few minutes everything seemed calm and relaxed.

- Children aren't born with the ability to calm the stress response in their underdeveloped brains.
- Children need warm, attentive and intentional parents to help them develop the capacity to deal with overwhelming stress situations later in life.

# The art of managing meltdowns and tantrums

*"I don't feel very much like Pooh today,"
said Pooh.
"There there," said Piglet. "I'll bring you tea
and honey until you do."*

– A.A. Milne, *Winnie-the-Pooh*

Meltdowns and tantrums are normal. All children have them. Contrary to what your friends or your interfering aunt may say, meltdowns and tantrums certainly don't mean that you are a bad parent or that your toddler has problems. They are related to your child's unique sensory temperament and developing brain, which means that some toddlers are more inclined to have meltdowns than others.

In short: the bad news is that you can't escape a meltdown or tantrum happening at least once while your child is growing up. But the good news is that once you know what a meltdown really is and you manage it correctly, you can reduce its occurrence, and make great things happen in your child's brain.

Your toddler turns two and you know that although this is a time when great things happen, you secretly can't help but fear the dreaded "terrible twos" – as it is so often called. However, I challenge you to replace the notion of "terrible twos" with "terrific twos". Change your frame of mind on what toddlerhood means – don't fear the worst, rather embrace this amazing, interesting, never-a-dull-moment time in your child's life. I assure you that once you understand the difference between meltdowns and tantrums and have some tools in your kit to manage them, there is nothing to fear.

Within the safe confines of my consulting room, desperate mothers have admitted that they feel completely out of control and desperate when their toddlers have a meltdown or a tantrum. Recently a mum exclaimed that she was seriously considering putting her toddler for sale on eBay … and she didn't look as if she was joking.

Let's be honest – we've all had moments of feeling like this.

## Meltdowns versus tantrums

Meltdowns and tantrums – *an intense storm of feelings* – could leave you and your toddler feeling overwhelmed, frightened, angry and at times very helpless. Some toddlers experience regular meltdowns, whereas others rarely have them. As hard as they are to manage, if you succeed, great things happen; over time your toddler will realise that it is okay to feel angry or frustrated, but that what we do with the feelings is important.

Managing meltdowns and tantrums is an art. In order to learn this intricate skill, you need to be able to distinguish between the two. Only then will you be able to manage them correctly.

The peak age for meltdowns is eighteen to twenty-four months, after which they occur less and less (but older toddlers, adolescents and even we as adults can have the occasional meltdown). At around two years toddlers' brains are flooded with intense feelings, but they don't always know what to do with them and how to calm themselves down when they get overwhelmed by big feelings. Poor impulse control makes it difficult for them to wait – if they want something, they want it *now*! They have huge needs and wishes, but they don't speak well yet and can't make themselves understood; this leads to irritation, frustration, arm waving, foot stamping, shouting and screaming.

Toddler meltdowns are often brought on by the little, unimportant things in life. That is, the things that seem little and unimportant to us; to them they are not little or unimportant. To them they are very real: having to share their favourite toy, having their play interrupted, having their toys packed away when they are busy creating something (even though they haven't created anything with the same blocks that have been spread across the floor for the past two days), having to get into the car strapped into their car seat, having to finish a meal in the high chair, having to get dressed in a warm jumper when all they want to do is wear their favourite sun dress. In the bigger scheme of things really not worth having a screaming fit over, but, to a toddler with an undeveloped brain, who is not yet able to see the bigger scheme of things, they are a really big deal.

Between three and four years, with your toddler's improved language skills, he is learning impulse control, his frustration tolerance is increasing and, owing to a more developed thinking brain, the frequency and intensity of his meltdowns will decrease. For some toddlers, however, the increase in the ability to use the thinking brain may lead to more deliberate and calculated behaviour. This may result in an increase in another type of challenging behaviour – not a meltdown caused by distress, but a tantrum caused by the desire to control and manipulate. Tantrums can increase if your toddler sees that they work, if he witnesses outbursts at home in the family or on TV, or if he has yet to develop the ability to calm himself down and respond in an appropriate way to big feelings such as frustration, anger and fear.

## The differences between a meltdown and a tantrum

| Meltdown | Tantrum |
| --- | --- |
| Occurs in toddlers of all ages, but mostly in the younger ones. It peaks at 18–24 months and sometimes increases again around three and a half years of age. | Occurs in the older toddler who is able to think realistically and behave in a calculated way. Behaviour is deliberate and about winning, getting what he wants. |
| Happens because your child is having difficulty processing sensory input and is overloaded by feelings of rage, fear, panic and separation. Even feel-good emotions like joy and excitement might cause dysregulation and a meltdown. | Happens in the older toddler if the meltdowns when she was younger were managed by time-outs, being ignored and/or sarcasm, resulting in your child never learning good self-regulation strategies. |
| Your child is overloaded – i.e. unable to talk and listen due to the fact that the primitive part of her brain is in the driving seat. | Your child is not dysregulated – he is able to talk and listen. |
| Your child often doesn't speak, doesn't make eye contact and sheds real tears. | Your child will speak and grunt, and usually makes eye contact while watching your reaction. There are usually no tears (although toddlers can force real tears). Your child negotiates or argues. |
| Your child cries or even screams uncontrollably. Some young toddlers cry but no sound comes out of their mouths. They often stop breathing for a few seconds when they suddenly get upset (when they're angry or get a fright). See the following box. | Your child's cries and screams are manipulative and sound forced. Your child screams "Waahhh!", then takes a breath, then screams again "Waahhh!", and breathes again. |
| Your child can be physically wild, kicking, hitting, throwing himself on the floor or throwing things. | Your child will be able to control his actions, e.g. will kick harder to try to get a response or make an impact. She will often throw things. |

| Meltdown | Tantrum |
| --- | --- |
| **Possible dangers when *repeatedly* mismanaged:** | **Possible dangers when *repeatedly* mismanaged:** |
| Your child will grow up struggling to deal with big feelings. | Your child will learn that she is able to bully or manipulate people and how to get what she wants. |
| Your child will cut off feelings such as pain and loss, due to the fact that he never learnt how to manage them when he was younger. | Your child will insist on instant gratification. |

**BREATH-HOLDING**

I never experienced this as a mother, but I've seen mums freaking out because their toddlers have stopped breathing – usually after a sudden fright or becoming really angry. It is frightening, but quite common. Some toddlers catch their breath and begin breathing after thirty to forty seconds, others pass out and then start breathing. You can help your toddler to start breathing by blowing directly into his face a few times or sprinkling cold water in his face. It might also be a good idea to call your doctor, especially if your toddler passes out and his body is twitching a little.

**MANIPULATION**

As a rule of thumb, young toddlers (younger than about eighteen months) do not have the mental capacity to think in manipulative ways. Their meltdowns are real and not a strategy to manipulate you to have their needs met. Older toddlers, however, whose parents consistently mishandled their meltdowns, might use manipulation and/or resort to a full-blown tantrum to get their way.

**GIVING IN VERSUS GIVING ATTENTION**

Parents may feel that they are giving in when they give toddlers much-needed attention during their out-of-control moments. The effectiveness all depends on *when* you are giving in and *when* you are giving attention. If you give your toddler attention when she is having a temper tantrum, then, yes, you are showing her that her manipulative behaviour will cause you to give in and, yes, she will use it again. But, very importantly, if you give your toddler attention when she is having a meltdown, she feels safe and understood. With time she will learn to manage difficult moments and big feelings on her own, without falling apart.

## The secrets of managing meltdowns

### Anticipate

Anticipate and, if possible, avoid difficult environments and situations that might lead to meltdowns. Close to nap times and meal times or the end of the day is *not* the time to run errands or to go shopping with your toddler. Being mindful of how you structure your day will reduce the likelihood of meltdowns dramatically. However, life doesn't stand still when we have toddlers, and there will be occasions when you don't have a choice and you have to go out with a fretful and tired toddler. This is how you do it:

- Keep the trip as short as possible (buy only the essentials that you need; the rest of your shopping list can wait).
- Give him big bear hugs.
- Talk less.
- Give your toddler a fidget toy to play with.
- Give him water from an exercise bottle and a crunchy snack like apple or carrots.
- Use calming sensory input (e.g. deep touch and sucking) and switch the thinking brain on (give your toddler a book to look at).

## Stepping in

- **Give appropriate and realistic choices**
  Don't offer too many choices; just say, "Would you like me to help you fix the tower that broke, or should we rather pack it away?"

- **The three-times-yes technique**
  This is one of the most powerful techniques and works nine times out of ten. It works like this: ask your toddler three questions or make three statements to which the answer could only be "yes". For example, she is refusing to get dressed and you can see that you are heading towards a meltdown. Say to her:
  "You want to stay in your pyjamas, don't you?"
  "You want to play for longer, don't you?"
  "You wish that you never had to get dressed, don't you?"

- **Distraction**
  Distraction is a wonderful strategy that switches on the thinking brain and turns off the primitive and emotional brain causing the meltdown. It also works well if you do it after the three-times-yes technique.

Two-and-a-half year-old Isabelle has a difficult time parting with toys at her crèche or friends' houses. In the past she would have a meltdown – she would hang onto the toy for dear life while her mum would be trying to pull it from her grip (you have to wonder what Isabelle must think about Mum grabbing from her, when Mum is always telling her not to grab from others). But her mum has learnt one of the secrets of managing meltdowns – how to anticipate and avoid the meltdown before it happens. Now, when it's time to leave she pulls Isabelle's favourite soft toy from her bag and says, "I know you want that toy, but we have to leave it here. Look, Bunny is calling you. He wants you to take him for a walk. He is hungry and we need to find him some food." She then quickly marches her off outside.

Be careful not to overuse distraction or use it to *prevent* your toddler from experiencing big feelings.

## Regulate

### CALM YOURSELF FIRST

Take deep breaths. This really works, putting the brakes on and slowing things down. Give yourself a minute or two. Close your eyes and concentrate on one thing and one thing only:

- Breathe in: fill your lungs with air.
- Breathe out: let all the air out.

*I know ... I know ... Shhh ... Shhhhh*

Let go of your feelings – your shame, guilt, anger and frustration. Even if you have to take yourself to another room – walk away, count backwards from twenty.

Remind yourself that you are the container for your toddler's big feelings. Remind yourself that your toddler will, with your help, feel calm again.

### GIVE HUGS OR JUST MOVE CLOSER

It is important to remind ourselves what physical closeness and touch do to our brains and bodies: they activate the release of calming hormones, which helps to restore balance. Put your toddler on your lap, bend down to his level and give him a big bear hug, or cradle him in your arms like a baby. Move closer; crouch down to his level, sit next to him or put your hand on his back.

### USE CALMING WORDS, BUT SPARINGLY

Lower the tone of your voice, speak slowly and say things like, "I know, I know", "Mum is with you, ssshhh" and "I'm going to hold you until you are calm again". Show empathy and acknowledge that you understand that her big feelings are real (at least for her, even if you can't understand why not being able to have another biscuit would warrant such an extreme fuss). Make your sentences short; do not give too much information or teach lessons on how to behave next time. You are meeting your toddler's emotional brain. You are acknowledging her feelings, which makes her feel that she is being heard, that she matters and that she is loved. This in itself is often enough to avoid meltdowns in all children.

Meltdowns are real for your toddler. Her frustration and disappointment (or whatever she is feeling) should be managed with **sensitive handling**. Your toddler needs *you* to help her restore calmness and develop ways to regulate and manage her big feelings. When you stay with your toddler, you are providing the container for her big feelings. This means that she feels safe and supported. (When adults act aggressively, violently and destructively, this is usually because they missed out on the parenting early in life that should have taught them how to manage their big feelings.)

# Time-in instead of time-out

When toddlers are in a state of overload, they are not able to make sense of what you say, to think clearly or to reason. Negotiating and lecturing your toddler during this phase is a waste of time. Talking and teaching need to happen **after** the storm – when your child is calm and attentive again.

Use the time-in technique when your toddler's behaviour is unacceptable, for example if he hurts another toddler or makes rude remarks, and you know that he is capable of knowing that his behaviour is wrong. This is done by asking your child to sit in a safe (but boring) place, such as a chair, a step or a kitchen bar-stool. In our house we call it "The Thinking Chair". Be specific about why you are using time-in: "I know it is difficult to share, but it is not okay for you to hit. I want you to sit here because in our family we don't hit other people." With an older toddler, "I want you to sit here and think about what you could do instead of hitting. In our family we don't hit other people." Don't give a long lecture – state the facts, set the limits and move on. Toddlers switch off if we give them too much information, and at this stage neither his brain nor his body is able to deal with information overload.

> "Talking and teaching need to happen *after the meltdown* – when your child is calm – not when he is *in the middle of the meltdown.*"

# If nothing works

If you feel disheartened, desperate, demoralised and isolated – that you've tried everything but you are unable to reduce the frequency of meltdowns or tantrums – consider the following:

## You might have reached your limits

Your high levels of stress might have worn you out and you need to look after yourself. Parents who are hedgehogs generally find it very difficult to deal with toddlers who moan, whine and cry, because of the noise. Looking after yourself and finding ways to regulate is very important (see page 144). You might need some me-time (even just for a few hours) or some exercise, so that the feel-good hormones (serotonin and endorphins) can be released and the level of stress hormones (dopamine and adrenaline) can be reduced. It is a good idea to seek comfort from your spouse or partner, your family or friends or even a counsellor.

## Your toddler may be in a developmental phase where things are a bit out of sync

Toddlers don't always develop in a predictable one-step-at-a-time pattern. Development happens in spurts and, when this happens, things will be out of balance for a while. Keep reminding yourself that the behaviour you are seeing now will not last forever. It, too, will pass.

## Your toddler might need more than just you

She may need a warm, attentive and supportive adult – to calm her and reduce the frequency of her meltdowns. If your toddler is demonstrating challenging behaviour that is affecting her development and her general functioning, she may have underlying sensory, social and/or emotional problems. You may need to consider consulting a paediatric neurologist and/or a health professional, specifically an occupational therapist who deals with sensory processing, or an educational psychologist for guidance.

# Successfully managing tantrums

Remember when your child is having a tantrum, he is using his thinking brain – mainly to get what he wants. His brain is not in a state of distress and therefore he doesn't need you to rescue him. What he needs is a very different approach. When dealing with tantrums you need to be calm, but firm. Follow these guidelines consistently when you are certain that you are dealing with a tantrum:

## Acknowledge feelings but discourage negative behaviour

We need to tell our children that we understand that they feel mad, sad, frustrated or excited and that these feelings are sometimes so overwhelming that they feel they might burst. But they need to find acceptable ways to express those big feelings. We therefore separate our children's feelings from their behaviour.

The message is: it is okay to experience the feeling, but we don't hit, bite, scream, push or grab in response.

Acknowledge feelings, but set the boundary for acceptable behaviour. You can say something like: "I know you really want another go on the swing but we don't push our friends off." With younger toddlers you might offer a choice: "Should we ask her if you could have a turn when she's done or would you like to go on the slide while we're waiting for a swing?" For older toddlers, ask open-ended questions such as: "If you want a turn on the swing, what do you think you can do?" Your child's response will indicate how much he's learnt about self-regulation. He might come up with ideas such as: "We could ask if we could have a turn"; "We could come back later".

Most of the time, this works. When it does, praise your child for good behaviour.

## If acknowledgement doesn't work

If your child's tantrum continues, your response will depend on your child's behaviour.

### Behaviour that doesn't cause hurt or damage

When the non-complying and defying behaviour, such as whining, shouting or kicking, continues (behaviour that doesn't cause any hurt or damage to himself or others), don't get into a battle and try to negotiate, reason or argue. Walk away, ignore and don't give more attention. Don't be tempted to blame, shame or humiliate. Simply set the boundary, state what behaviour you expect, then ignore the child. Walk out of the room or walk away from the place where he is throwing a hissy fit. This might be difficult, especially in public places. Just remember the bigger picture. You are working towards having a well-regulated child. Big feelings are okay, but it's not okay for children to disobey purposefully, or to manipulate or to insist on always getting their way.

## Behaviour that could cause hurt or damage

When destructive, calculated behaviour that hurts others and/or damages property continues (or starts), use time-out. Always use this as the last resort. Time-out involves taking the child away from the situation and putting him on the "thinking chair" or in a room. Tell your child: "You are doing time-out because it is not okay to punch your brother. You will stay in there for … minutes." Allocate one minute for every year of age; for example, a four year old will have four minutes in the room or on the chair. Once the time is over, go back to step one: acknowledge the feeling, but state the expected behaviour.

**Important facts about meltdowns and tantrums**
Certain facts are vital for you to know when it comes to meltdowns and tantrums.
- Both are an essential part of growing up, although there are times they certainly can be avoided.
- Meltdowns and tantrums are *not* the same thing. They have different underlying reasons, your toddler behaves and responds differently, and they most certainly need to be handled differently.
- Meltdowns occur in the younger toddler and peak between eighteen and twenty-four months, when your toddler's brain is flooded with intense feelings, but he doesn't yet have the language skills or the thinking skills to manage them.
- Meltdowns occur less and less in older toddlers. Occasional meltdowns are due to tiredness, hunger and overstimulation after a long day, which sends the primitive feeling brain into overdrive.
- As toddlers grow and develop, meltdowns occur less frequently, but three-year-olds, school-aged children, adolescents and even adults have them from time.
- When you manage meltdowns and tantrums correctly, your toddler learns important life skills (how to deal with feelings of disappointment, frustration, resentment, humiliation, anxiety, anger and loss of control).

# PART IV

·····································

# Intentional
# parenting tools

# Nurturing rituals and predictable routines

*"One of the advantages of being disorganised is that one is always having surprising discoveries."*

– A.A. Milne, *Winnie-the-Pooh*

All children need nurture to survive and routine to thrive. Some children need more than others because of the unique way their brains are wired, their unique sensory temperament. As with all things, too much routine and overdoing the nurturing side of things may reduce a child's ability to engage with the world, but too little causes havoc. Rituals and routines – whether it is playtime, nap time, eating time, daddy-coming-home time – add an element of predictability (which is particularly important for hedgehogs and monkeys) and help to bring a sense of calm to the chaos that comes with our busy lives.

*"The younger the child, the more they gain their sense of security and emotional stability from the predictability of an established routine."* Anne Cawood

Some people thrive on routine and rituals. The sense of sameness and predictability helps them to stay calm and focused. Others tend to avoid it as much as possible because they feel it might compromise their creativity. Whatever your thoughts, I'm sure you will agree that, to some extent, routines and rituals do exist in your life. In essence, they are just *activities that happen at about the same time and in about the same way each day.*

## Why have nurturing rituals and predictable routines?

Most children benefit from rituals and need a flexible routine, because:

- **It makes them nicer to be around**
  Kids that follow routines are easier to "read" because their signals are usually linked to specific times in their routine. When they are getting grumpy and you check your watch, you'll find that it probably is close to lunch time or nap time. There is some predictability to their behaviour, and as a result they are less demanding and challenging.
- **They learn how to regulate themselves**
  If children have a time for sleep, they learn what it feels like to be drowsy, asleep and awake. If they have set meal times, they learn how their body feels when it needs food or something to drink. They experience the thrill of running around and then calming down for meal time. Through rituals and predictable routines children learn the basics of self-regulation. "If my body is like a car engine, then it runs fast when I'm playing and slows down when I'm sleeping. So next time Mummy says it is sleep time, I'll know what my body feels like" (Mary Sue Williams and Sherry Shellenberger: *How Does Your Engine Run? Leader's Guide to the Alert Program for Self-Regulation*).

## The nuts and bolts of rituals and routines

In order for rituals and routines to be sustainable and to work they should be family specific. What will work for me might not work for you. Bearing the following in mind may help you when considering why some of your routines and rituals are working and others are not.

- Create routines that consist of a **scheduled set of activities**. For example, bathtime and bedtime include a set of activities: bathing (having a little play in the bath), putting on pyjamas, brushing teeth, story time (reading two stories) and bed time (cuddle and light off).
- Create routines that are **flexible** (while still being predictable). If the routines are too rigid, children don't learn to be flexible – an important life skill. Routines need to be flexible within themselves – the set of activities (bath, story, bed) stays the same, but perhaps once a week bathtime can be postponed for some gentle rough-and-tumble play when Dad comes home from work. As your child gets older, routines also become more flexible because they have to make space for other family members and their needs too.

**EXAMPLES OF PREDICTABLE ROUTINES**

- Morning routines – helpful to get everyone ready for the day, out of the house and on their way to daycare, playgroup, crèche, school and work
- Meal-time routines
- Bedtime routine – from babies to grannies, as this sets the stage for a good night's sleep

**EXAMPLES OF NURTURING RITUALS THAT WORK**

- Good morning rituals – wake up with a kiss, cuddle in your bed or whatever works for your family
- Good night rituals – say a prayer, kiss on the cheek, sing a night-time lullaby
- Family meetings
- Family nights
- Birthday celebrations
- Christmas
- Holidays – having a bucket list of "10 things we would like to do"

## Helping children deal with changes in routines

Although as intentional parents we might strive to create nurturing rituals and predictable routines, life happens and there will be days when your toddler has to deal with changes in your routines. You may feel ill and not able to drop him at the nursery school on your way to work, there may be road works forcing you to use a different route to get home, bathtime took longer and now you only have time for one story. The way your child deals with the changes in the rituals and routines is hugely dependent on his unique sensory temperament.

Sarah, our sensitive little **hedgehog** (see page 49), thrives on routines and rituals. She does not like changes. She likes to wear the same clothes, sit in the same chair at the dining room table and eat the same food. She complains when her mum has to change her bed linen and insists that her room never be moved around. She is not "shy" to let others know about her likes and dislikes and will *really* let everyone know if she's not happy with what is happening – she moans, complains, has meltdowns and turns everything into a drama. (Not all hedgehogs will let us know that they don't like changes; they might respond by "curling up into a ball", and withdrawing.) Then we have Jack and Jonathan who respond very differently to changes in their routines and when asked to adapt to new things. Jack, the **monkey**, embraces it and loves the prospect of new people and new places, but the danger is that he could become overstimulated. Jonathan, the **giraffe**, doesn't seem to be bothered at all.

Rituals and routines help hedgehogs feel safe by increasing the predictability in their lives. To some extent they can become overly dependent on them, which makes it really hard when things do change, when they have to stop one thing to do another, or when they need to make transitions from one environment to another. Unfortunately for hedgehogs, life is full of changes and transitions. They may need some support and practice in learning how to deal with change without becoming overwhelmed. Not only is it a part of life, but it's also important for the developing brain. New connections and pathways are established when we participate in new, unfamiliar activities and when we are exposed to new situations. Learning happens in that space between comfort and discomfort. Too much comfort results in stagnation, whereas too much discomfort creates stress and anxiety. I love this quote from Michael Hyatt: "… the really important stuff happens outside your comfort zone".

## Tips for dealing with transitions and change

- **Play, play and play some more.** As busy parents, we can't be available for play twenty-four hours a day, but we do need to make time for playing with our toddler. Let him take the lead. Let him decide how you will play and the rules of playing. In this way, his feelings of control and security increase, which helps to carry him through the times when he is faced with uncertainty.
- **Play unpredictable games.** When children play games that force them to deal with the unexpected, during times when they are feeling happy and calm, they learn to become more flexible. Musical chairs, duck-duck-goose and snakes and ladders are useful for developing more flexibility within the child. Often hedgehog toddlers avoid playing these types of games. Take extra care to be loving, warm and empathetic in your approach when encouraging them to join in.
- **Humour** is a great way of reducing tension and anxiety, and a powerful tool during transitions. Pretend to be a bedtime fairy that is going to take your child to her room. At meal times, go down on all fours and pretend you are a dog who is hungry and needs food. These types of interactions switch on your child's thinking brain, overriding the primitive feelings that make transitions difficult. In most cases your child will join you in this playfulness, resulting in a smooth transition.
- **Focus on the unchangeable.** Point out things in his life that will not change and that will stay the same. Even though the child might be moving to a different house, he will continue to attend the same school, all his toys and his bed will stay the same and his dog is coming along too.
- **Make use of familiar objects** like a favourite blankie or soft toy to ease anxiety during transitions. A new environment and experience, such as the school or the dentist, will be less scary if your child can cling onto something comforting and familiar.
- **Give control over the uncontrollable.** When kids resist changes, or struggle to make the transition from one activity to the next or from one environment to another, they often feel powerless. Give her some power back; show her that she can "win" by giving her choices, especially in the little things that mean such a lot to a toddler. Choose your words carefully and say things such as: "We have to turn the TV off now. Would you like to push the button to turn it off or should I do it?", "We need to go home now. Do you want to press the button on the lift or should I do it?" or "We need to get dressed now. Would you like to choose what you will wear or should I choose for you?" Make sure that the choices you offer are relatively exciting, or this might backfire. Saying something like, "We have to go and bath now. Do you want to tidy the toys away or should I do it?" will most certainly not work!

- **Prepare in advance.** Letting children know what is going to happen next makes their lives more predictable. And with predictability comes more control and less fear or anxiety or defiance. Most of us love being in control, and children are no different. Giving advance warning of what is going to happen will help your toddler to make the transition from *now* to *then*: "I'm having breakfast. After that I will go to school." You might want to try the following to support your toddler:
  - ◀ **Visual schedules** can include pictures and basic sight words to describe the different activities. Be creative – stick them up in a row from left to right on the fridge, put Velcro strips or dots of Prestik on the back of the pictures and let your child take each one off and post it in a box when that activity is completed. The more active and involved your child is when doing visual schedules, the greater the impact.
  - ◀ **Timers** work well to indicate that it is time to stop. They are great to use when sharing – each child gets a few minutes to play with a certain toy, then when the timer goes or the sand runs through it's the other one's turn. Because it is not *you* saying that it is time to stop (or time to go or time to get changed or whatever), there is less likelihood of arguments and the child seldom blames you.
  - ◀ **Verbal reminders** involve you saying what you are expecting to happen. "We need to leave in five minutes", "When you've finished reading that book, we have to go home", "When that programme is finished, we need to turn off the TV", "When you've finished your juice, it is time for a nap", "When we've finished reading the book, it is bedtime", "When you've pushed me over five times, it is time to stop our rough-and-tumble game." And then be sure to make it happen! A fun way is to make a trumpet sound to announce what's coming next.
- **Give praise.** Remember to notice when your child is able to make a transition well and give positive remarks. "You got out of the bath so quickly. Wow, that's amazing!"

> "Learning happens in that space between comfort and discomfort."

# 12

# Intentional discipline

·····································································

*"If the person you are talking to doesn't appear to be listening, be patient. It may simply be that he has a small piece of fluff in his ear."*

– A.A. Milne, *Winnie-the-Pooh*

The word *discipline* is derived from the Latin word *disciplina*, which means "teaching" or "training". It doesn't mean to punish or to reprimand. It is not about controlling our children, or forcing our will onto them. Discipline and boundary setting, when done respectfully, are about *teaching* our children how to behave.

We want our children to behave appropriately not just because of the fear of being caught – that is not what self-regulation boils down to. You want your child to think, *I'd better not grab Johnny's toy because grabbing is rude*, rather than, *I'd better not grab because I will get into trouble*. There are excellent resources available that deal extensively with this topic and from which I've learnt a great deal. However, I find that most of the books fail to consider the following when talking about behaviour management, discipline and boundary setting:

- Young children have immature brains, which mean they are still in the process of learning how to control their bodies, calm their big feelings and decide on the best way to manage situations.
- Children have unique sensory temperaments and therefore respond differently to boundary setting and discipline.

So I've set out to give you an age-appropriate guide for boundary setting that relates to your unique child. Discipline and boundary setting have been extensively researched and documented. For centuries, psychologists and developmental specialists have researched and hypothesised about the effect of different discipline styles on children and their socio-emotional development. One thing remains certain: children need to be disciplined – *taught* – in the right ways of life.

## Discipline doesn't mean

Misperceptions regarding discipline include the belief that a warm and attentive parent is the opposite of a parent who sets boundaries and disciplines a child. The truth is ***all parents should set boundaries, but in a warm and attentive manner***. Often parents fall in two camps: the "anything-goes" parent (with excessive giving-in tactics) and the "tough-love" parent (who is excessively controlling). Both parenting styles place unrealistic expectations on a developing child with a developing brain, and do not tap in to the child's unique temperament – often with devastating effects.

> "Intentional parenting is not about *whether* you set boundaries; it is about *how* you set them."

# Discipline means

To raise great kids, parents need to **set clear boundaries and provide guidance and structure**, consistently and **in a warm, attentive and flexible way**. Depending on your child's unique sensory temperament, he may need *fewer* or *more* boundaries. Intentional parenting is not about *whether* you set boundaries; it is about *how* you set them.

# A hand of support

Imagine your child crossing a stream of water by stepping on well-placed rocks. At times you will hold his hand to support him while he strides from one rock to the next. At other times he will move from rock to rock without any support from you. This is exactly how the process of boundary setting unfolds. We need to be attentive – available to provide a hand of support when our child needs it, but also willing to let it go when he succeeds in managing the challenge without support. Too much support and too much control will discourage your child from learning new skills, while too little support will result in him making too many mistakes without effective skill development.

  The reality is that as parents we are not always there to provide just the right amount of support at just the right times. And frankly, we don't always have the capacity and the ability to do it either. The truth is we don't always have to be. Our children will learn a great deal from the times that we are not there, but we don't want them to "drown" either. So here's the challenge: finding the balance between providing support and letting go.

## Intentional boundary setting

Within our relationship with our children, we need to let them know: "I will keep you safe" and "I will make sure that you are okay". Boundaries need to be consistent and age appropriate. Only then will children feel safe and be able to develop self-regulation as it applies to:
- their bodies and actions (stopping before grabbing the toy)
- their feelings (not being overwhelmed by big feelings)
- their thoughts (thinking of ways to respond, e.g. walking away, asking for a turn).

The two things in which you need to be consistent are: **Empathising with your child's emotion** without **condoning inappropriate behaviour**.
  Most well-intentioned parents make a few common mistakes when setting boundaries:
- We set them when we are angry.
- We set unrealistic boundaries.
- We are inconsistent about following through on the boundaries.

We often find ourselves in a situation where we either do too much of the one or too little of the other. Imagine the following everyday situation.

David and Sarah are playing while their mums are having tea. David grabs his favourite toy from Sarah and in the process hurts her a little. David's mother thinks, *Oh no, he grabbed the toy from Sarah. But it is his favourite and Sarah didn't ask if she could play with it, so he's probably upset.* She does nothing, while David walks away with the toy in his hand and leaves Sarah feeling confused and near tears. A moment later the same thing happens, but this time Sarah grabs the toy from David. Sarah's mum responds by pulling her aside, telling her off for grabbing the toy and enforcing a two-minute time-out.

Both mothers were reasonably attentive – at least by being aware that something had happened. However, neither of them managed to deal with this situation in a way that builds relationships and social-emotional development. David's mum succeeded in understanding where David's behaviour was coming from, thus showing some empathy, but this was not accompanied by any boundary setting for his behaviour. Sarah's mum, on the other hand, managed to set boundaries for the behaviour, but without warmth and empathy.

## Showing empathy and setting boundaries

The ideal response in this situation would be for David's mum to say, "David, I know it is your toy, but we do not grab from our friends." Then she should give David some time to process what she's just said. If he doesn't respond by handing the toy to Sarah, then say, "Give it back to Sarah please. When she has finished playing with it, you can have a turn." By adding the last sentence, she is helping him to learn to delay his need for instant gratification, as well as providing an incentive for good behaviour. She empathised with his feeling and she set the boundary. If you always do this in the same warm and attentive way while staying calm, your child will feel heard and he will feel safe. If your child does not respond as you expect him to, if he grabs the toy again, he may need you to step in and with a firmer hand. If this pushes him into a meltdown, calm him down before proceeding with your "teaching" and boundary setting. Children respond differently to boundary setting, which depends to a large degree on their unique sensory temperament.

# Boundary setting and sensory temperaments

Some children need a firmer hand when it comes to boundaries, and some need a softer, warmer approach, no matter what age they are.

**Hedgehogs** are sensitive and highly attuned children. They often know what the rules are without you having to spell them out repeatedly. If they don't follow the rules then they only need gentle reminders. Hedgehogs are also better at developing impulse control than monkeys. When you tell them to stop, they will, most of time. When they see an interesting object on the table, they will think of the consequences before picking it up. Of course, hedgehogs also need boundaries, as there will be times when they do break the rules – which often happens more within their familiar environments than at school or at friends' houses.

Use this guide for boundary setting for sensitive children:

| Avoid | Do more |
|---|---|
| • Yelling, as many hedgehogs are sensitive to noise | • Use the softest voice you can muster |
| • Forcing your child to make eye contact and stay close to you while you reprimand; your hedgehog's brain is flooded with stress hormones during a reprimand and in an effort to keep it all together and regulate her actions and emotions she may look away and fidget | • Reprimand in private or a little way from where the action and the crowd is |
| • Physical punishment, e.g. spanking | • Allow older toddlers to choose their own consequence |
| • Shaming, i.e. punishing her in front of others | |
| • Withdrawal of love | |
| • Isolating | |

**Monkeys**, on the other hand, are risk takers, thrill seekers and boundary pushers. They will need even more consistent, more rigid and less flexible boundaries.

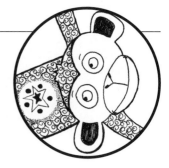

# Reminders about boundary setting

## Find good behaviour

So often we focus on the behaviour that we don't want to see or things that we don't want to happen. We say things like, "Don't play with the ball in the house." When you see "good behaviour" – behaviour that shows your child's ability to self-regulate, for example calming himself, making easy transitions, controlling himself and showing kindness – make sure that you point this out to him. "I'm proud of you; you shared your toys today", "You were smart today. It was a good idea to go to your room when your friends were making too much noise", "Great! It is helpful when you use your words to tell me that you are angry".

Children in general respond better to *earning* privileges than having privileges *taken away*. This gives them a greater sense of control – the ball is in their court. This works well with older toddlers who are more advanced in the development of self-regulation than younger tots. Put a marble in a jar every time your child is able to demonstrate self-regulation, for example using his words to express his big feelings. When the jar is full, he can have a treat. Remember: the younger the child the smaller the jar should be, so that he can be rewarded more quickly. Children love treats that include spending time with you (reading a book or playing a game), as well as treats like sweets, special outings or screen time.

## Don't expect your toddler to take a reprimand and boundary setting gracefully

This is a good reminder for me too, as my expectations are often far too high. Remember that your overall goal with disciplining and boundary setting is to teach your toddler, who is behaving from a primitive brain perspective, ways to control her body, feelings and thoughts. But this process takes time and practice. Kicking, screaming, hitting, cursing and temper tantrums are not acceptable. However, try your best to ignore her pulling an angry face (which is currently my little hedgehog's favourite way of showing her annoyance and frustration with my boundary setting), muttering under her breath, moaning or saying, "It's not fair!" Take a few deep breaths, turn your back and focus on your own self-control. (No name calling when someone cuts you off on the road!)

# Age-appropriate boundary setting

No matter how old your child is, you will be spot-on if the boundaries have the following goals:
- Keeping safe
- Showing kindness to others

This means nothing that will compromise the safety of and respect for the child and others.

## Very young toddlers (eight to eighteen months)

From the time when your baby starts actively interacting with you and the environment, you must help him understand that we are living in a world where he can't just do whatever he likes to do. From the age of about eight months, a baby starts learning about right and wrong, and that his **behaviour carries consequences**. At this age babies and toddlers are able to start interpreting your facial expressions, but they do not always do this consistently. Your frown and the vigorous shaking of your head might be met with a smile and laughter … frustrating for you when you are actually trying to say, "Stop what you are doing!"
- Be consistent – make sure your gestures and tone of voice are appropriate for the words you are saying. Don't wave your finger, frown and say, "No spitting" when he spits his food in your face, but laugh the next time he does it.
- Reinforce what you are saying by removing your toddler from the situation and/or by using distractions.
- Do this over and over again in the same way. Remember the goal of boundary setting and discipline: we *teaching* our kids and them *learning*, and that takes practice.
- When you consistently enforce the boundaries, it is highly unlikely that your little one will need any more than that.

## Young toddlers and older toddlers (eighteen months to five years)

Toddlers need **concrete rules**, such as, "No pinching. That hurts." They need to understand that we treat other people with respect, which includes, "We share" and "We don't shout", and we treat objects with respect: "Walls are not for drawing on. Paper is." Teach your child how to get what he wants while respecting others: "You wanted to play with the ball too. You may not grab. When you want the ball, ask for a turn."

Toddlers also need some extent of **control**. Give choices, two positive choices as a way of setting boundaries but also giving them an opportunity to stop and think (therefore working on the wiring of the thinking brain). "It is time to get dressed now. Would you like to wear the red or the blue T-shirt?", "It is bathtime. Would you like to play with the bubbles or should we get the shaving cream?", "We're going now. Would you like me to strap you into the car seat or do you want to do it by yourself?", "Are you taking a book or a toy along to the shops?" and "Remember I read two stories at bedtime. Would you like to go and choose them?" For older toddlers, you can start introducing more complex problem solving: "We cannot jump and shout in the house. You can jump and shout outside or you need to stop. What do you want to do?"

# Boundary setting within a strong connection

Setting boundaries and disciplining our children can only be effective or take place in the context of a strong connection and relationship with them. I've seen thousands of kids who act out, behave badly and behave in challenging ways, sadly because they've lost the connection with their parents. Of course there are other reasons for challenging behaviour as discussed in Chapter 10, but the breakdown of the parent-child connection is often a contributing factor.

**Let's change the way that we discipline by bearing in mind:**
Discipline means to teach. It involves being warm, attentive and flexible when setting age-appropriate boundaries that keep in mind our child's unique sensory temperament.

Our goal with boundary setting and disciplining is to teach our children how to regulate their feelings, thoughts and actions. This involves much more than just obedience and compliance. It needs to come from within. When our children know what it means to *be calm* rather than just how to *act calm*, we are well on the way to raising calm, connected and happy children.

# What about *you*?

> *"Love is taking a few steps backward (maybe even more) ... to give way to the happiness of the person you love."*
>
> – A.A. Milne, *Winnie-the-Pooh*

Caring for a child's physical needs and emotional wellbeing can take its toll. Most parents have a difficult time balancing the needs of others (especially those closest to them) with the need to nurture themselves. The flight attendant who tells us that in an emergency we need to put our own oxygen masks on before assisting others has a good point. As parents we need to look after ourselves. It is important. It is vital. Nurturing yourself means that you are kind to yourself, you love yourself and you believe that you are enough. It is only when we love ourselves that we are able to love our children and connect with them in a deep and meaningful way. Joseph Chilton Pearce writes: "What we *are* teaches the child more than what we say, so we must *be* what we want our children to become."

In this chapter it is time for me to get onto my soapbox and preach what I believe lies at the core of being an intentional parent. As much as I'm laying out the foundations for you, they serve as reminders to myself.

Merely holding your breath and coming up for air from time to time is not sustainable on this parenting journey. In this section we will take a look at the three steps that will help you feel that you are wearing an oxygen mask at all times from which you can get your strength and courage:

- looking after yourself;
- looking after your world; and
- enjoying the journey.

# Looking after yourself

Parenting is one of the most demanding jobs there is and often it is not your only job. Juggling a career, parenting, housework, marriage, family commitments and friendships is hard work, and finding time for yourself while keeping all the balls in the air can be challenging. Let's be honest: the demands on modern parents are extraordinary, and there will be times when you feel exhausted, resentful and discouraged.

 **1** Focus on healthy eating

Chemicals and hormones work together to regulate our mood and enhance our ability to think logically. Eating specific foods produces feel-good hormones (serotonin and dopamine), which will enhance your quality of sleep, stabilise your mood and lower your stress hormones.

- Eat foods that make you feel good. Bananas, whole-wheat bread, pasta, oily fish (such as sardines, salmon, fresh tuna and mackerel), avocados, vegetables, nuts, cheese, baked potatoes, chicken and beef all release the feel-good hormones. Busy parents should also take a daily dose of a good quality vitamin and mineral supplement. This includes supplements rich in vitamins B6 and B12, fish oil and flaxseed oil.
- Never skip breakfast or lunch. Non-breakfast eaters are likely to feel depressed and anxious. Breakfasts are designed to *get* you going and lunches to *keep* you going. Breakfast should consist of complex carbohydrates (e.g. oats) and include a protein and a fat (e.g. milk or yoghurt), which will make your blood-sugar levels rise slowly for a few hours – providing you with sustained energy and stabilising your mood. Lunches should be high in protein (fish, chicken and lean meat, nuts and cheese) to keep you going, focused and alert for the rest of the day. If your lunch consists mainly of carbohydrates, you may feel sleepy during the afternoon owing to the drop in blood-sugar levels (a lesson for all of us who tend to grab a sandwich).
- Snack on fruit or protein. Make up snack packs to grab on the run. If you do this in advance, you will be less likely to reach for sugary biscuits, salty crisps and caffeine-rich tea and coffee.
- Drink six glasses of water each day. Keep a jug or a water bottle filled with water. For variety, add mint, cucumber, lemon, fruit tea or natural berry elixir.

**2** Exercise

Walk, run, cycle, swim, dance – do whatever works for you, but be deliberate and make time for exercise at least three times per week. Exercising releases feel-good hormones, such as endorphins and serotonin. Goal-directed movement and heavy work (proprioception) organise our brains and bodies, stabilise our mood and keep us focused and attentive. You can do cycling, swimming, power walking, jogging, rowing, Pilates, yoga, kick boxing, aerobic classes, weight

### Jungle juice

This drink is great for an energy boost. Mix the ingredients and keep it in your fridge. When you've had a sleepless night, or if you have a hectic day ahead, drink two litres in the course of the day to help you keep going.

*Mix the following ingredients:*
1 litre apple, grape or berry juice
1 litre water
50ml Herbaforce Schlehen Blackthorn Berry Elixir

*Optional:*
– 1 sachet Blackcurrant Rehidrat or Raspberry Electropak (add this if you are breastfeeding)
– 1 dissolvable vitamin tablet, such as Berocca or Redoxon (add for increased energy; note that this will replace your daily vitamin supplement)
– 8–10 drops of Bach Rescue Remedy or Bach Rescue Night

The main active ingredient of Jungle Juice is the Schlehen Blackthorn Berry Elixir, which is available at leading health and baby shops (even taken alone, this will give you a boost of energy; mix one tablespoon in a glass of water or a cup of rooibos tea and take three times daily).

training, Zumba – the list goes on and on. Find something that fits your sensory profile and your lifestyle. If you are a monkey, you will benefit from high-intensity, heavy-work exercises that are goal-directed, such as cycling, Zumba, kick boxing, rowing and jogging (you can add some ankle or wrist weights to increase the proprioceptive input). A giraffe will benefit from high-intensity aerobics, Zumba or kick boxing with loud music. Hedgehogs do well to make time for power walking, jogging, Pilates, yoga, aerobics, rowing and weight training.

## 3  Derive strength from doing things you enjoy

The things that you enjoy doing are usually a good fit for your unique sensory temperament, so do more of them. They will give you joy and regulate you, which will carry you through the rough times. If you are a sensory craver (monkey), you might enjoy social interactions and entertaining but find you lack the energy and time to invite friends over for a dinner party. Be realistic: don't host a three-course dinner party, but invite your friends for a simple one-pot meal. Host mother-and-baby or mother-and-toddler groups at your home, or try to attend a weekly stimulation class. The contact with other mums and children will suit your sensory temperament. On the other hand if you are a sensitive person (hedgehog), you might be challenged by the unpredictability of children, the lack of consistent routines and their behaviour. If you've always enjoyed being alone for creative activities, make sure you build time for this into your lifestyle. Go for a walk in nature and experience the beauty around you.

**4  Use positive self-talk**

Negative thoughts are detrimental to our physical and emotional wellbeing. Positive thoughts, on the other hand, create brain cells that are filled with proteins, which enrich the body and brain, giving us a new release of energy and health. Instead of thinking, *I'm such a terrible mum, I lost it again with the kids today,* you can say to yourself, *It's okay to make mistakes. I'm not supposed to be a supermum all the time.*

**5  Ask for help and accept help offered**

The African saying "It takes a village to raise a child" is so true. However, modern families aren't always fortunate enough to have access to the "village" or community to help carry the load. We may live miles away from the nearest family, and since we are all busy mums we feel guilty when we ask for help, or we are too proud to accept help when it's offered. Brené Brown has challenged my thinking on this subject by saying: *"We can't give help if we can't ask for it."* If you can't ask for it, it means that you are judging those who ask for help. For those of us who are keen to offer help to others but not asking or accepting help, that is a difficult pill to swallow. I urge you to accept help from anyone who offers it, in whatever form – whether it is making you a cup of tea, doing some of your ironing, taking the kids to school, picking up groceries or preparing a meal. Have the courage to ask your spouse, neighbours, friends and family members for help, even if they don't offer. Practise being vulnerable. Once again Brené Brown explains it best: *"Vulnerability is not knowing victory or defeat, it is understanding the necessity of truth; it's engaging."*

## Looking after your world

### Be realistic

Most of us are all too fond of making "To do" lists. It might be a good idea to replace the phrase "To do" with "I want to" or "I would like to". The reality is that, as mums, we don't get to do half the things we did before we had kids. Don't be unrealistic and set yourself unattainably high standards – feelings of frustration and resentment, even guilt and shame, will set in. I've come to realise that a realistic goal for me is to attempt to get three things done in a day. Some days those three things might be:
- Ensure they are dressed before leaving for school.
- Ensure they eat at least one of their five fruits and veggies.

- Give each of them a cuddle and say "I love you".

Easy! That means that everything I get done over and above those three is a bonus. I can get into bed at night and give myself a *high five*. I did it!

## Start saying "no"

We live in a society that has become increasingly self-centred, which means that people often say "no" because they are either too busy with their own lives or have been told that, in order to reduce their stress, they have to start saying "no". And I hate that. That said, you might find you are the one that can't say "no". There will be times in your parenting journey when the first priority has to be you and your family. When you feel that you are over-committing and need to reconnect, this might be the time when you need to start saying "no" – graciously. Be intentional about your priorities and the goals you have set yourself as a parent. Remember that you, and only you, know what is best for you and your family.

# Enjoying the journey

## Stop comparing

It is not fair on you or your family to compare your parenting style and/or your children with anybody else's. No two families are the same, and comparisons could result in resentment, unrealistic expectations and anxiety setting in. What good can it do to say to yourself, *I'm not as good a mother as so-and-so because my children don't listen to me the way hers listen to her* or *Her children are doing music, drama, swimming, art and karate. I need to get my child to these classes too, or he'll fall behind or feel left out*?

Deciding with your spouse on what is important to you as a family is a good way of developing your own identity, and lends purpose and direction to your family (without the need to compare with other families). Write a "mission statement" that defines your purpose and values. This will add value to your intentional parenting journey.

It also needs to be said that the flip side of *stop comparing* is *stop judging*. Your family and your children and your values and your situation differ from that of your neighbour, your friend around the corner, even your sister. What I've learned through the years is that there is not one single parenting strategy or parenting approach that has all the answers. There are thousands of great parents and great kids out there and I bet that when we ask them, they wouldn't all be using the same approach and have the exact same parenting values. We need to practise how to honour differences and respect the choices that our friends are making when it comes to how they parent.

## Live in the moment

Work hard at being content in the current season of your parenting journey. I found this especially difficult when my children were younger because I felt that there was very little time for doing the things I wanted to or even had to do, like paying bills and writing thank-you cards. But the truth is that if you are wishing the season away, you are less engaged in what is going on in the moment. This means you are less attentive and less able to be the warm and engaging mum that your child needs. When you are pushing your toddler for the hundredth time on the swing, enjoy that very precious moment. Replace all the thoughts of, *I could have made that call to the bank and prepared the supper by now* with *I am so privileged to be here in this moment with my child*. How many times has your mother told you to enjoy the time you have with your kids because it will be over in a flash? She is right. Before we know it our children will be all grown up and leave home. We need to keep reminding ourselves about the importance of living in the moment.

## Be real and give up perfection

I've said this many times before. There is no such thing as a perfect parent, or a perfect child for that matter. The sooner we stop trying to be perfect, the better. Be real with feelings such as shame, isolation, anxiety, fear, depression, worry, frustration and exhaustion. Admit that it is difficult and that you don't get it right all the time every time. Stop controlling. Stop putting lids on difficult emotions. Allow things to get messy. Parenting perfection is not the goal.

"A deep, meaningful relationship with our children is what matters most. Love with your whole heart even if there is no guarantee."

# FINAL WORD

*"Sometimes, if you stand on the bottom rail of a bridge and lean over to watch the river slipping slowly away beneath you, you will suddenly know everything there is to be known."*

– A.A. Milne, *Winnie-the-Pooh*

Parenting in the 21st century would definitely be much easier if we knew everything there was to be known. All I know is that we know very little. Each day scientists and researchers are discovering more about how our brains and the events we are exposed to affect our development, our relationships and our behaviour. I am convinced that we will never see the day when we can say we know everything there is to be known.

That doesn't mean that we should stop learning and trying to be the best parents we possibly can. I strongly agree with Stephen Covey, who wrote in his book *Seven Habits of Highly Successful People*, that we have to "begin with the end in mind". We have to ask ourselves the question: "Who is the person I want my child to be when he is older?" Parents all over the world want their children to be happy and joyful and live a purposeful life, have meaningful relationships and contribute to society in a significant way.

Our society places less importance on a high IQ and innate ability than in the past, and these qualities are less likely to define a person's success in life and career.

Our children will be confronted by far greater challenges throughout their childhood than we've ever had to face. Qualities that they weren't born with will be critical for their happiness and success in life; these qualities develop through the interactions and experiences that we as parents provide, nurture and encourage. Your child will develop these qualities and thrive once he has mastered the skills of regulating his body, feelings and thoughts.

Your child's ability to *self*-regulate is the *foundation* on which complex social, emotional and cognitive development is built.

# Two golden rules for raising happy children

## Remember that your child's brain is in the process of developing

In fact, until your child is five years old, her brain is fairly primitive and out of balance. The thinking part of her brain is incomplete. This will affect her behaviour hugely in terms of her ability to:

- control her impulses and delay the need for immediate gratification
- sustain her attention
- deal with big feelings, such as frustration, rage, fear, separation, distress and joy
- understand language and use words to name her feelings.

## Know your child's unique sensory temperament

The way in which your child deals with sensations underlies his temperament. Is your child a **monkey** – social, alert and on the move; a **giraffe** – laid-back, easy and adjustable; or a **hedgehog** – sensitive, attentive and thoughtful? Knowing your child's temperament will help you understand his behaviour, tune in to his needs and manage challenges along the way. It will help you to figure out what causes him to stress and what helps him to stay calm and alert. Your monkey might need more opportunities for purposeful and goal-directed movement, your hedgehog will need a den that she can use of time-in and your giraffe will need lots of movement and sounds to get him going.

# REFERENCES

Aron, Elaine N. 2002. *The Highly Sensitive Child: Helping our children thrive when the world overwhelms them*. London: Thorsons.

Ayres, A. J. 2005. *Sensory integration and the child*. Los Angeles: Western Psychological Services.

Bailey, B.A. 2001. *Easy to love, Difficult to discipline: The 7 basic skills for turning conflict into cooperation*. William Morrow Paperbacks.

Bailer, D.S. & Miller, L.J. 2011. *No Longer a Secret: Unique common sense strategies for children with sensory or motor challenges*. Texas: Sensory World.

Biel, L. & Peske, N. 2005. *Raising a Sensory Smart Child: The Definite Handbook for Helping Your Child with Sensory Integration Issues*. New York: Penguin.

Bryson, Tina Payne & Siegel, Daniel J. 2011. *The Whole-Brain Child: 12 Revolutionary Strategies to Nurture Your Child's Developing Mind*. London: Constable & Robinson Ltd.

Brazelton, T. Berry. 2006. *Touchpoints: Birth to Three – Your Child's Emotional and Behavioral Development*. New York:Da Capo Press.

Bronson P.O. & Merryman, A. 2009. *Nurtureshock*. UK: Ebury Press.

Brown, B. 2012. *Daring Greatly: How the courage to be vulnerable transforms the way the live, love, parent and lead*. London: Penguin.

Cawood, Anne. 2009. *Toddlers need boundaries: Effective discipline without punishment*. Welgemoed: Metz Press.

Chapman, Gary & Campbell, Ross. 2005. *The 5 Love Languages of Children*. Chicago: Northfield Publishing.

Covey, Stephen. 1997. *Seven Habits of Highly Effective Families*. London: Simon & Schuster.

Eliot, Lise. 1999. *What's Going on in There? How the Brain and Mind Develop in the First Five Years of Life*. New York: Bantam.

Faure, M. & Richardson, A. 2008. *Baby Sense*. Welgemoed: Metz Press.

Fraiberg, S.H. 1996. *The Magic Years: Understanding and Handling the Problems of Early Childhood*. Scribner.

Frick, Sheila M. & Colleen Hacker (2001). *Listening with the Whole Body*. Madison, WI: Vital Links.

Galinsky, E. 2010. *Mind in the Making: The Essential Life Skills Every Child Needs. Volume One*. William More Paperbacks.

Gold, M. G. 2011. *Keeping your Child in Mind: Overcoming Defiance, Tantrum, and Other Everyday Behaviour Problems by Seeing the world through Your Child's Eyes*. New York: Da Capo Press.

Goleman, Daniel. 2011. *The Brain and Emotional Intelligence: New insights*. Northampton MA: More than Sound.

Greenspan, S.I. 2000. *Building Healthy Minds: The Six Experiences that Create Intelligence and Emotional Growth in Babies and Young Children*. New York: Da Cabo Press.

Greenspan, S.I. & Greenspan. J. 2009. *Overcoming ADHD: Helping your child become calm, engaged and focused without a pill*. New York: Da Capo Press.

Greenspan, S.I. 2007. *Great Kids: Helping your baby and child develop the 10 essential qualities for a healthy happy life*. New York: Da Capo Press.

Green, C. 2006. *New Toddler Taming: The world's bestselling parenting guide fully revised and updated*. UK: Vermillon.

Karp, H. 2004. *The Happiest Toddler on the Block: How to eliminate tantrums and raise a patient, respectful and cooperative one-to-four-year-old.* New York: Bantam Dell.

Kranowitz, C. 2005. *The Out-of-Sync Child: Recognizing and Coping with Sensory Processing Disorder.* New York: Perigee.

Kranowitz, C. 1995. *101 Activities for Kids in Tight Spaces.* New York: St.Martin's.

Kranowitz, C. & Newman, J. 2010. *Growing an In-Sync Child: Simple, fun activities to help every child develop, learn and grow.* New York: Perigee.

Lombard, A. 2007. *Sensory Intelligence: Why it matters more than IQ and EQ.* Welgemoed: Metz Press

Miller, L. 2006. *Sensational Kids: Hope and help for children with Sensory Processing Disorder.*

Ratey, John J. 2001. *A User's Guide to the Brain.* London: Abacus.

Richardson, A. 2005. *Toddler Sense.* Welgemoed: Metz Press.

Serena Wieder & Harry Wachs. 2012. *Visual/Spatial Portals to Thinking, Feeling and Movement.* Profectum Foundation.

Shure, M.B. 1996. *Raising A Thinking Child: Help your young child to resolve everyday conflicts and get along with others.* New York: Pocket Books.

Smith, K.A. & Gouze, K.R. 2005. *The Sensory-Sensitive Child: Practical solutions for out-of-bounds behaviour.* New York: HarperResource.

Sunderland, M. 2006. *The Science of Parenting: Practical guidance on sleep, crying, play and building emotional wellbeing for life.* London: Dorling Kindersley Limited.

Williams, Mary & Shellenberger, Sherry. 1996. *How Does Your Engine Run?® A Leader's Guide to the Alert Program® for Self-Regulation.*

# INDEX

# ACKNOWLEDGEMENTS

**Thank you.** A phrase too short for the gratitude I feel towards those who've been part of this journey.

I'd like to thank the following people from the bottom of my heart (if I have missed anyone, please know that it was not intentional):

- My husband, Marius, for being one of the most intentional dads on this planet. When my self-regulation fails me, you are the one who hugs me, tells me to breathe and reminds me that it's okay if things get messy. I am so thankful that you are the one who walks beside me and holds my hand on our parenting journey. I'll choose no one else.
- My extraordinary girls, Lize and Cara. I thank God each and every day for the miracle of having you. You teach me, you inspire me, you humble me, you encourage me, you freak me out and you love me. Your excitement about my message keeps me going. I love you most!
- My dad and mum, Louis and Jena. Thank you for teaching me the importance of relationships and showing me how to love.
- My siblings and extended family who are all amazing, Cobus and Liza, Jean and Charlotte, Louise and Stephen. Thank you for your love and support.
- My parents-in-law, Faan and Magdel and sister-in-law, Adéle. Thank you for your unconditional love and being totally crazy about our girls.
- My niece, Firn Hyde. Your first edit on a very rough draft helped me find my voice in ways that you'll never know.
- My dear friend and colleague, Marese Brink. Your support, encouragement, help and advice are deeply woven into this book. I'll always be grateful that our paths crossed the way they did.

Lots of friends, colleagues and fellow mums took the time to read, give advice, write an endorsement or a review. I don't want to omit anyone and I truly hope that you know who you are. Special thanks have to go to Marietjie Schoeman, Melanie Peek, Marna Esterhuizen, Helen van Staden, Kim Arnold, Robyn Stephenson and the girls on the launch team who cheered loudly.

Gratitude goes to the Metz Press team who made one of my dreams a reality. Thank you Wilsia, for believing in my message and showing remarkable patience with me on this first-time journey of writing a book. When I felt vulnerable to the bone your final edit gave me the courage to carry on. To Lesley Hay-Whitton for the first edit and for your words of encouragement. To Louise Vorster for not leaving a single word untouched while doing the translation into Afrikaans. It was fun scratching heads with you on word choices. To Nikki Miles for the illustrations. Thank you for giving me a glimpse into your creative mind and meeting with me in the beautiful Stanford. To Liezl Maree for hearing my heart and making this a beautiful book.

I would like to thank the pioneers and leaders whose work provided the backbone for this book: The late Dr. Stanley Greenspan, Dr. Lucy Miller and Margot Sutherland.

And then there are those whom I admire and who have, without knowing, challenged me to dare greatly: Megan Faure, Hettie Britz, Annemarie Lombard, Marga Grey, Michael Hyatt, Lysa Terkeust, Ann Voskamp, Brene Brown, Dr. Caroline Leaf.

My acknowledgements cannot be complete without me thanking God, our everlasting Father. I've felt your presence throughout this journey. I thank you for your grace, kindness and goodness, and for the joy of motherhood.

# PRAISE FROM PARENTS AND PROFESSIONALS

Raising Happy Children *is a magnificent book with an important message for parents and professionals – drop the super parent/ super professional cape and embrace humility and vulnerability. Being understood by an adult is essential for a child to grow and change. Lizanne manages to empower adults in helping them understand children from a sensory perspective.*
**Sanet Schoeman, Educational Psychologist**

*In an ever evolving society where it is increasingly important to foster the capacity in children to relate, engage and be "socially savvy", Lizanne maps the way in a very clear and concise manner to empower parents. A "must read" for any intentional parent.*
**Karin Buitendag, Occupational Therapist and Clinical Director of Occupational Therapy, Sensory Processing Treatment and Research (STAR) Center, Denver, Colorado**

*Parenting today is difficult and daunting within a busy, overloaded and fast-paced world. We need all the help we can get to take daily steps in nurturing, loving and guiding our children to be happy and healthy.* Raising Happy Children *is a practical, easy-to-understand and insightful book that will not only make you as a parent feel more capable but also prepare your children to become resilient adults.*
**Dr Annemarie Lombard, Occupational Therapist, Founder and CEO Sensory Intelligence® Consulting, author of** *Sensory Intelligence, why it matters more than IQ and EQ*

*Neither as a therapist, nor as mom, have I ever been so encouraged and inspired by a parenting book. Lizanne transforms one of the most daunting and complex tasks into a wonderful journey, with all the empathy, guidance and tools that one needs to feel confident about raising happy children. What a generous gift to all parents!*
**Nancy van Zyl , Occupational Therapist and mom of two**

*Lizanne combined her passion for neuro-science and children in a remarkable way by bringing us Raising Happy Children. She draws from her vast experience as therapist and mother to illustrate the theoretical concepts that form a solid base for this book. Her deep compassion for parents shines through this work. I can't wait to share this with some of my clients.*
**Nita Lombard, Occupational Therapist**

*Feeling overwhelmed by all the parenting "guides" available? Look no further ...* Raising Happy Children *will empower you as parent by not only giving you a full understanding of your child's behaviour, but also provide you with many practical strategies to deal with discipline, routines, meltdowns, conflict, emotions, and their unique sensory temperament.*
**Leana Matodes, Speech Pathologist, author of** *Time2Play*, **New South Wales, Australia**

*Understanding the difference between meltdowns and tantrums has transformed the way that I parent my toddler.*
**Helen, mother of Ralph**

*Lizanne says it all! I enjoyed every page from the title to the last sentence. Raising Happy Children is a tool to use towards happy children AND happy parents. I'll recommend this book to parents with children with special needs but also to parents in general, including my own children, to ensure happy grandchildren.*
**Marga Grey, Occupational Therapist, author of** *Sensible Stimulation* **and** *Sensory Motor Skills: Functional Implications*, **Developer of CoordiKids programs, Queensland, Australia**

Raising Happy Children *bridges the gap between a book for therapists and a parenting book. Lizanne has managed to transform complicated concepts into readily understandable, practical and fun information that will change the way that you parent forever.*

**Marese du Preez, Occupational Therapist and new mom on the parenting journey**

*Lizanne has masterfully, yet humbly, brought the complexity of parenting, the human body and relationships together. As much as this book is meant for parents of typically developing children, I would recommend it to all my parents of the children that I see in my practice. This book will take the stress out of parenting and will make it a fun and enjoyable experience.*

**Ray Anne Cook, Occupational Therapy, Chairperson of the South African Institute of Sensory Integration**

Raising Happy Children *is one of the most practical and insightful parenting books I have ever read. It makes so much sense and I'm wondering why I never saw my children's behaviour from this perspective. Reading this book has helped me to understand myself, my husband and my children better. And love them even more.*

**Sarah, Mother of Jonah and Katherine**

*They say that babies don't come with a manual, yet Lizanne has managed to explain important neuro-developmental concepts in a concise and comprehensible way that will help every parent understand their child better. But she doesn't stop there! Her practical strategies and real-life examples will help you get the best out of your children and really enjoy family life.*

**Melanie Peeke, Parenting Practitioner at ADD-vance, London, UK**

*In this book Lizanne succeeds being both vulnerable and helpful. The insights she shares throughout the book gave me permission to be the parent I've always wanted to be. I now know who my child really is and feel more equipped to manage challenging behaviour we might face in the future.*

**Tamzyn, Mother of Jack**

*Lizanne writes in a wonderfully conversational way ... demystifies complex concepts for parents and gives practical tips to help you transfer knowledge into practice. This is one of those books that you will refer to on regular occasions and not leave on the bookshelf to collect dust! This book has encouraged us to be more present and more intentional in the way we parent our little ones and will be a helpful tool both professionally and personally.*

**Lourdes Bruwer and Carly Tzanos, Occupational Therapists, authors and moms**

*Lizanne's book is full of fun and practical advice to help parents navigate the often confusing world of rearing children. As a parent of a "hedgehog" and a "monkey", I have found that her sensory based-approach has been incredibly effective in helping me to understand my children's needs (and increase harmony at home!). It should be essential reading for every parent who's ever stood in a supermarket watching their child meltdown in public!*

**Kim Arnold, Mum of Hope and William**